W9-CBF-584

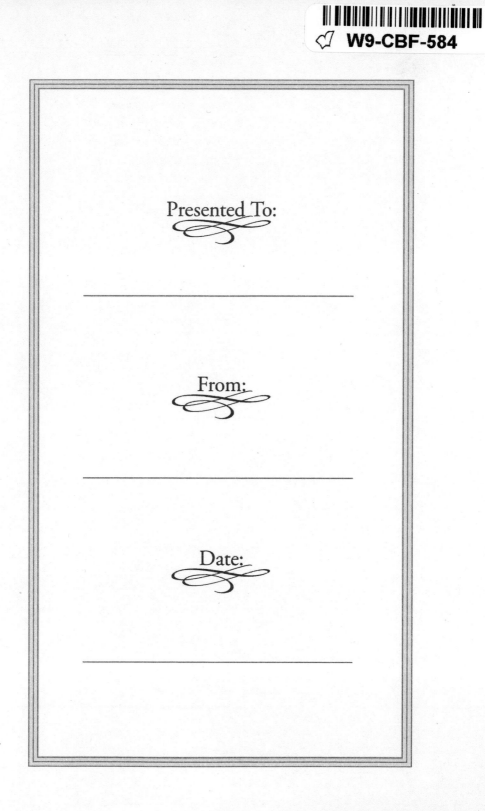

Presented To:

_____

From:

_____

Date:

_____

LADY
IN
WAITING

DESTINY IMAGE BOOKS BY JACKIE KENDALL AND DEBBY JONES

Lady in Waiting: Devotional Journal and Study Guide
by Debby Jones and Jackie Kendall

Lady in Waiting: Meditations for the Heart
by Debby Jones and Jackie Kendall

The Young Lady in Waiting: Developing the Heart of a Princess
by Jackie Kendall and Debbie Jones

Lady in Waiting for Little Girls by Jackie Kendall and Dede Kendall

Lady in Waiting Student Edition by Jackie Kendall and Debby Jones

Raising a Lady in Waiting: Parent's Guide by Jackie Kendall

The Right Guy for the Right Girl by Jackie Kendall and Debby Jones

The Mentoring Mom: 11 Ways to Model Christ for Your Child
by Jackie Kendall

A Man Worth Waiting For: How to Avoid a Bozo by Jackie Kendall

Free Yourself to Love—The Liberating Power of Forgiveness
by Jackie Kendall

LADY IN WAITING

Becoming God's Best While
Waiting for MR. RIGHT

JACKIE KENDALL
AND
DEBBY JONES

© Copyright 2014– Jackie Kendall and Debby Jones

All rights reserved. This book is protected by the copyright laws of the United States of America. This book may not be copied or reprinted for commercial gain or profit. The use of short quotations or occasional page copying for personal or group study is permitted and encouraged. Permission will be granted upon request. Unless otherwise identified, Scripture quotations are taken from the NEW AMERICAN STANDARD BIBLE®, Copyright © 1960,1962,1963,1968,1971,1972,1973,1975,1977,1995 by The Lockman Foundation. Used by permission. Scripture quotations marked NIV are taken from the HOLY BIBLE, NEW INTERNATIONAL VERSION®, Copyright © 1973, 1978, 1984 International Bible Society. Used by permission of Zondervan. All rights reserved. Scripture quotations marked KJV are taken from the King James Version. Scripture quotations marked NLT are taken from the Holy Bible, New Living Translation, copyright 1996, 2004. Used by permission of Tyndale House Publishers, Wheaton, Illinois 60189. All rights reserved. Scripture quotations marked PNT are taken from *The New Testament in Modern English*, J. B. Phillips, trans., Copyright © New York: The Macmillan Company, 1960. All rights reserved. All emphasis within Scripture quotations is the author's own. Please note that Destiny Image's publishing style capitalizes certain pronouns in Scripture that refer to the Father, Son, and Holy Spirit, and may differ from some publishers' styles. Take note that the name satan and related names are not capitalized. We choose not to acknowledge him, even to the point of violating grammatical rules.

DEDICATION

We dedicate this book to all the Ladies in Waiting, especially our daughters Jessica, Christen, and Lauren, who are seeking to become women of God… *and my (Jackie's) incomparable writing mentor, Ruth A. Olsen.*

CONTENTS

PREFACE

If you're anything like me, you have an outfit (or two…or three…) hanging in your closet that is somewhat outdated—but it remains there because it is a *classic!* Maybe it's a perfect dress for an evening wedding or even just your very favorite pair of jeans and cozy sweater. One day, however, you take a really honest look at that outfit and you just *know* it needs updating. It still fits and it still looks really good…but it needs to be freshened up and, frankly, brought into the current decade of style.

With that cute dress, you might take off the sleeves and add a little ruffle around the skirt hem. Maybe you'll pair it with some new shoes and completely different jewelry next time you wear it. And as for the jeans, well, isn't it time you had a denim maxi-skirt? You get my point. There are classics that are really well made, but from time to time, they need an update. That's what we're doing here with *Lady in Waiting;* she's getting altered just enough to showcase her timeless principles in a 2014 fashion.

What we did with this *20th Anniversary Edition* of *Lady in Waiting* was update and enhance: update some of the material to enhance the principles in the book that are time-tested. So you will see lots of new illustrations and added examples woven right in with the original text. While embellishing the best-selling classic, it's not a complete overhaul. This is to say there are a number of issues that have become HUGE in our culture among singles since twenty years ago: Internet dating, social media temptations, same-sex attraction, pornography and other sexual taboos (like dating married men), to name a few.

We are not addressing these *directly* in this new edition, but absolutely every principle to guard and guide the *heart* that applied to single gals twenty years ago applies now. The particulars do not alter the principles.

Whether you're thirteen or thirty, in these pages you will find so many transferrable concepts that impact whatever situation you are facing now. More than that, if God's best for you is to marry, these principles hold true then. In fact, whenever I hear about a woman's struggle—single, married, or divorced— most of the time I can trace the issue back to one of the precepts in this book that was not applied. After almost forty years of marriage, I want to shout on national news that the concepts in this little book were the foundation of building a marriage that remains upright, secure, and sure while so many marriages around us have collapsed!

May this *20th Anniversary Edition* become an invaluable resource for you as *you* become a *Lady in Waiting* upon the Lord, our great and holy and loving Lord God.

INTRODUCTION

Is this just another book for singles? No! We believe this book is unique because its emphasis is not on a woman's status (single, married, divorced, or widowed), but on the state of her heart. We want to direct a woman's attention toward the One who really understands the longing of her heart. Too many women grow up believing that the inconsolable ache in her heart is for "a man." To love a man, get married, and then have children is thought to be the only script that will satisfy her heart's deepest longing. But no man, woman, or child can appease this longing; it can only be satisfied by the ultimate Bridegroom, Christ Jesus. This book nudges a woman closer to God, while acknowledging any longing she may have to be loved and cherished by a man.

Lady in Waiting is not about finding the right man, but being the right woman. Thus it focuses on ten qualities of a godly woman that are found in the Book of Ruth. These qualities will not only enhance your love relationship with your heavenly Bridegroom, but also guide you as a single woman, guard you while you date, support you in marriage, and comfort you if you are ever widowed or divorced. As you read you will see these characteristics beautifully displayed in the life of Ruth. She recklessly abandons herself to the Lordship of Christ, diligently uses her single days, trusts God with unwavering faith, demonstrates virtue in daily life, loves God with undistracted devotion, stands for physical and emotional purity, lives in security, responds to life with contentment, makes choices based on her convictions, and waits patiently for God to meet her needs.

A FAIRY-TALE ENGAGEMENT

When my Boaz was planning to propose to me, he wanted to do something unique and memorable. He put a lot of thought and effort into making our engagement one of the most treasured times of our lives together! To this day when I remember all the special details he attended to, as well as the ways that the Lord blessed that beautiful night, I am overcome with gratitude—and no small degree of awe (but I will get to that later).

In this age of reality TV shows about over-the-top engagements and weddings, when high-schoolers rent helicopters to stage the big "ask" to the prom, and first dates get taken to five-star restaurants, my story may not seem so extraordinary. But let your mind wander back to the mid-1970s when life was genuinely simpler and few American teens would have even rented limos for the prom. In *that* context, consider a college-aged young man who came out of a household of all boys and let me tell you what he planned and pulled off—all for the sake of getting to marry me! (Even typing that brings a lump to my throat.)

While we were home on break from our junior year of college, Ken made arrangements for us to drive to Disney World for the day. Just going to Disney World was a thrill for me—and is to this day! But Ken had much more in store than taking me up Space Mountain; he had called ahead and made reservations to take me to one of my favorite places in the world, Cinderella's Castle, and to a special restaurant inside the castle.

Can you even imagine how excited I was to walk through those doors and be escorted into the castle? I already felt like a princess with my attentive prince.

That was only the beginning of the night's surprises. After returning to the table from a trip to the restroom, our enchanted dinner was suddenly enhanced by a troupe of singing waiters, serenading us with songs about our love and delivering with a flourish a flaming order of cherries jubilee! As if this were not spectacular enough for this young woman in love with this wonderful young man, one of the waiters approached me with a beautiful book of poetry and declared, "A delivery from the prince of the palace!" It was a book addressed to "Princess Jacqueline."

And *then,* at what seemed to be the climax of this fabulous evening, our waitress asked, "Are you ready for me to take the picture?"

"What picture?" I blurted out, surprised again.

My sweet prince smiled at me and said, "She is going to take our picture out on the balcony overlooking the Magic Kingdom."

Well! If you think I walked, you'd be wrong, since I'm sure that I floated out onto that balcony. I knew full well that "no one" ever got to go to that special place—or, so it seemed—no one besides Cinderella waving at the crowds below. But there I was, and there we were, and before I knew it, the picture was snapped, the waitress departed, and Ken Kendall turned to me and asked me to marry him.

Was this really my life? For a girl from an abusive background, fairy tales and daydreams were a common way to disassociate from the painful world I lived in. How utterly ironic it was that in such a magical place, Ken would ask me to be his bride. How utterly fitting, as well: Walt Disney himself was raised in an abusive home and dreamed of creating a beautiful, fun, and safe place for families. Out of something painful in his life, he created something beautiful: Disneyland and Disney World. Out of something painful in my life, God was creating more beauty than I could imagine.

The very night of our engagement, God gave Ken and me a special bonus that shone with *His* beauty. As we left the castle, we both remarked about Jan, our waitress, and how open she seemed to spiritual things. She made several remarks during our wonderful dinner about her search for life's purpose. We shared as much as we could with her as she served our dinner, and now it seemed right to us to go back into the restaurant and tell her that we would love to talk with her more about this spiritual purpose in life that she was searching for. She accepted our invitation, said she got off work at 11 p.m., and told us that if we would come back, we could chat for a few moments.

Ken and I walked around the Magic Kingdom reveling in our brand-new status as an engaged couple, and anxiously looking forward to sharing with Jan about the reason she met us that night. When we walked back into the restaurant, Jan actually came running down the stairs to meet us! We sat in the lobby of Cinderella's Castle and shared with her the hope that we both had found in Jesus. She remarked, "You guys were so loving toward me, I knew there was something different about you both."

So that night, Jan bowed her head and gave her heart to Jesus as Savior and Lord. When we hugged her good-bye and turned to walk away down Main Street, we both said at the same time: "We just got engaged and we just led someone to a personal relationship with Jesus!"

It was the *perfect* ending to this fairy-tale night. Talk about double joy!

We walked out of the Magic Kingdom absolutely overflowing with joy. As we drove back to West Palm Beach, we prayed that God would use our wedding ceremony as profoundly as He'd used our engagement on the balcony of Cinderella's Castle. Indeed, in His faithfulness and power, He did just that.

A man named Bill, who was suffering with leukemia, attended our wedding. He was so touched by our ceremony that he made a point to share his feelings with someone at the wedding reception. That someone was my mother-in-law.

As guests left the reception, Bill stayed behind and Esther Kendall explained to Bill how he could know Jesus intimately the way Ken and Jackie shared in their special wedding ceremony. Bill bowed his head that day and asked Jesus to be his personal Lord and Savior. Our prayer the night we got engaged was answered with Bill's decision to accept God's gift of eternal life through Jesus. Bill died two weeks later. He was ready for Heaven, and God had graciously used our wedding as the scenario for his eternal decision.

THE GROOM COMES FOR HIS BRIDE

The part of the wedding ceremony that absolutely rocked Bill to the core was when all the bridesmaids had arrived at the front of the church and it was time for the bride to walk down the aisle. The preacher stepped to the microphone and said, "Just as someday Jesus will come for His Bride, the Church, even so today, Ken comes for his bride, Jackie."

You see, my father would not come to my wedding. In fact, if you can even imagine it, he told me to pick a replacement for him. Somehow I was given the wherewithal to say to my abusive father that there is no replacement for fathers. Yet it didn't matter. He was completely unwilling to budge. So, Ken and I prayed about how to handle this highly unusual and very painful situation.

Here is what the Lord brought to our minds: Jesus Christ will someday return and come for His Bride, the Church. Then, this remarkable young man of only twenty-four years responded with an idea replete with the grace of God: "Jackie, I will come and get you and bring you down the aisle."

I am quite sure that neither of us had ever seen such a thing, but it was a work of God through the man He prepared to honor and care for me in this way. Not only did it display tenderness and touch the heart of Bill, but several of our friends from broken homes went on to conduct their ceremonies the same way. In fact, thirty-six years later, our own son walked from the front of the church to meet his precious bride and escort her down the aisle…another chapter in this extraordinary fairy tale.

Before you throw down this book in anger that you didn't have this "fairy-tale" engagement story, and before you roll your eyes, dismissing such a sentimental scene, I ask you to take a small glimpse at the backstory of my life. The miracle of this whole experience, and of writing the best-selling book *Lady in Waiting,* is the painful context of my life. I am the oldest of seven children, all sexually abused by our father. The fallout was horrible—including two suicides of my siblings and lives destroyed in myriad ways.

So for me to learn in the Book of Ruth godly principles that guarded my heart and kept me from marrying a "Bozo guy"—that is a blessing I enthusiastically share with any woman who has a pulse! (Oh! And though many readers know this, for those who don't, the key character, the leading man in the Book of Ruth is named *Boaz.* And, as you can see, if you change one little letter in his name, he can go from a winner to a Bozo.)

A nurse I once met said to me, "It is amazing to think that someone from your background would pick such an awesome husband."

Well, amazing and awesome are attributes of God, and surely *His* hand was the guiding force in my very ability to marry my Boaz.

**Anything other than a love relationship with
the Lord Jesus Christ, regardless how good that thing may be,
will bring you discouragement and disillusionment.**

What are *you* waiting for? Is it for that perfect job, the ideal relationship, a home, a career, a child? What if you get what you are waiting for? Will it truly bring the fullness of joy you long for? Anything other than a love relationship with the Lord Jesus Christ, regardless how good that thing may be, will bring you discouragement and disillusionment. So come and explore the life of Ruth and learn what it really means to be a godly woman, "a lady in waiting."

Chapter 1

LADY OF RECKLESS ABANDON

Reckless abandon is a level of surrender that unlocks the greatest treasures God has in store for His kids. —JMK

The big day is over. Your roommate married a wonderful guy, and you were the maid of honor. You shared your roommate's joy, but now you wrestle with envy's painful grip. As the happy couple drives to the perfect honeymoon, you sit alone in an empty apartment, drowning your envy and self-pity with a half-gallon of Heavenly Hash ice cream.

Does this scenario sound familiar?

Have you assumed that your ultimate fulfillment would be found in marriage? Have you privately entertained the notion that the only satisfied women are married women? Have you been expecting your career to satisfy you until you are married? If you have answered "yes" to any of these questions, then you have a prospect of disillusionment looming in the future. On the back cover of the book *Learning to Be a Woman* is a key quotation about fulfillment as a woman:

A woman is not born a woman. Nor does she become one when she marries a man, bears a child and does their dirty linen, not even when she joins a women's liberation movement. A woman becomes a woman when she becomes what God wants her to be.[1]

This priceless truth can help keep your perspective clear in relation to true fulfillment in life. Too many Christian women think that the inner longings of their heart relate only to love, marriage, and motherhood. Look a little closer and see if that longing isn't ultimately for Jesus. Gary Chapman once remarked in a sermon:

> I feel very strongly that marriage is not a higher calling than the single state. Happy indeed are those people, married or single, who have discovered that happiness is not found in marriage but in a right relationship with God.

Fulfillment for a Christian woman begins with the Lordship of Christ in every area of her life.

A college professor (wife, mother of seven children, singer, and author) told a group of young women that when she was eight years old, her mother told her a secret that has guided her perspective on life. The most important thing her mother would ever tell her was, "No one, not even the man you will marry one day, can make you happy—only Jesus can." What a profound statement for such a little girl. This secret allowed her to grow up following Jesus with reckless abandonment.

Are you still convinced that having Mr. Right will chase away the blues? That's not surprising. On the front of a national magazine, the lead story said, "Hollywood's hottest newcomer is selling more records than Madonna and filling her dance card with movie offers. All that is missing is *Mr. Right!*" Such a mindset bombards singles daily. How can you renew your mind and rise above this stereotype? You can be an exception through understanding "the secret of the alabaster box."

THE SECRET OF THE ALABASTER BOX

In the days Jesus was on earth, when a young woman reached the age of availability for marriage, her family would purchase an alabaster box for her and fill it with precious ointment. The size of the box and the value of the ointment would parallel her family's wealth. This alabaster box would be part of her dowry. When a young man came to ask for her in marriage, she would respond by taking the alabaster box and breaking it at his feet. This gesture of anointing his feet showed him honor.

One day, when Jesus was eating in the house of Simon the leper, a woman came in and broke an alabaster box and poured the valuable ointment on Jesus' head (see Mark 14:3-9). The passage in Luke 7 that refers to this event harshly describes the woman as *"a woman in the city who was a sinner"* (Luke 7:37). This woman found Jesus worthy of such sacrifice and honor. In fact, Jesus memorialized her gesture in Matthew 26:13 (see also Mark 14:9). This gesture had such meaning, for not only did she anoint Jesus for burial, she also gave her all to a heavenly Bridegroom. Yes, she was a sinner (who isn't, according to Romans 3:23?), but this sinner had dreams and wisely broke her alabaster box in the presence of the only One who can make a woman's dreams come true.

Have you been holding on tightly to your alabaster box of dreams, frantically searching for a man worthy of breaking your box?

What is in your alabaster box? Is your box full of fantasies that began as a little girl while you listened to and watched fairy tales about an enchanting couple living happily ever after? Have you been holding on tightly to your alabaster box of dreams, frantically searching for a man worthy of breaking your box? Take your alabaster box to Jesus and break it in His presence, for He is worthy of such honor. Having responded to your heavenly Bridegroom in such a manner, you can wait with confident assurance that, if it be God's will, He will provide you with an earthly bridegroom.

How do you know if you have broken your alabaster box at the feet of Jesus? Such a decision will be reflected in reckless abandonment to the Lordship of Jesus Christ. When the Lord gives you a difficult assignment, such as another dateless month, you receive His terms without resentment. Your attitude will reflect Mary's response to the angel when she, as a single woman, was given a most difficult assignment. Mary said, *"I belong to the Lord, body and soul...let it happen as you say"* (Luke 1:38 PNT). Take your alabaster box, with your body, soul, and dreams, and entrust them to Jesus. When He is your Lord, you can joyfully walk in the path of life that He has for you.

RUTH'S RECKLESS ABANDONMENT

In the Book of Ruth, a young widow made a critical decision to turn her back on her people, her country, and her gods because her thirsty soul had tasted of the God of Israel. With just a "taste," she recklessly abandoned herself to the only true God. She willingly broke her alabaster box and followed the Lord wherever He would lead her.

> *But Ruth said, "Do not urge me to leave you or turn back from following you; for where you go, I will go, and where you lodge, I will lodge. Your people shall be my people, and your God, my God"* (Ruth 1:16).

As you look at the following three areas of Ruth's life that were affected by her reckless abandonment to God, consider the parallels to your own price tag of commitment to God. Have you broken the valuable alabaster box yet?

NEW FRIENDS

When Ruth told Naomi, *"Your people shall be my people,"* she understood that she would not be able to grow closer to the God of Israel if she remained among the Moabites (her own people). Ironically, God called Moab His washbasin (see Ps. 60:8; 108:9). One rinses dirt off in a washbasin. Ruth chose to leave the washbasin and head for Bethlehem, which means the "house of bread."[2]

Even today there exist "Moabites" who will undermine your growth if you spend too much time with them. Sometimes mediocre Christians resist the zeal and commitment of a dedicated single woman. Realizing that your friends drive you either toward or away from God, you may need to find a "new people" who will encourage your growth and not hinder it. *"He who walks with the wise grows wise, but a companion of fools suffers harm"* (Prov. 13:20 NIV).

Often the choice for deeper commitment produces resentment from people who were once "such good friends." Do not be alarmed; you are in good company. When the woman broke the alabaster box and poured it on Jesus, the disciples did not applaud her act of worship. Instead, with indignation they responded, *"Why this waste?"* (Matt. 26:8 NIV). The disciples of Jesus were filled with indignation because the woman obviously wasted the ointment. But from a heavenly perspective, the great cloud of witnesses rejoiced as they beheld the woman giving such honor to Jesus. The broken alabaster box publicly evidenced the woman's reckless abandonment to Jesus. Is there such evidence in your daily life?

**Be careful if you spend most of your free time
with a girl friend who does not share your commitment
to Jesus. It can affect your relationship with the Lord.**

This is not to advocate that you distance yourself from all who have not broken their alabaster box at the feet of Jesus. Just consider the ultimate influence your friends have on your commitment to the Lordship of Jesus Christ. Be careful if you spend most of your free time with a girl friend who does not share your commitment to Jesus. It can affect your relationship with the Lord. If non-Christians or lukewarm Christians influence you rather than you influencing them, you may be headed for serious trouble. You mirror those who influence you. When a woman stops growing spiritually, the lack of progress can often be traced back to a friendship that undermined her commitment to Jesus.

Take a moment to think about the spiritual depth of the girl friend who influences you the most. Is she daily becoming all that Jesus desires? If so, her growth will challenge you to grow. On the other hand, her apathy may ultimately be contagious. *"Do not be deceived: 'Bad company corrupts good morals'"* (1 Cor. 15:33). Have any of your friendships caused your spiritual life to go into a deep freeze?

Maybe you, like Ruth, need to distance yourself from those who, spiritually speaking, are more like a washbasin than a house of bread. The friends who influence you the most should be women who live by Hebrews 10:24 (NIV): *"And let us consider how we may spur one another on toward love and good deeds."* Your best friends should be cheering you on in your commitment to Jesus.

NEW SURROUNDINGS

Ruth had to relocate in order to be fed spiritually. Likewise, some single women may have to "relocate" because some of their former relationships keep them in a constant state of spiritual "hunger." They have to change jobs or even their church in order to continue to grow. In the same way, be open to a change that may benefit your spiritual growth. Like Ruth, look for something that will stimulate your growth in the Lord.

One young woman had to make a choice between playing on a championship volleyball team or being part of a discipleship group. She knew that she was free to play volleyball if she wanted. But when she compared volleyball and the discipleship opportunity, the Lord showed her that the good often becomes the enemy of the best in life. Because of her reckless abandonment in following the Lord's leadership, she valued her growing commitment to the Lord more than playing volleyball, and it paid off. The discipleship training prepared her heart to respond to an invitation to serve as a short-term missionary in the Philippines. Another young woman may be called to spend her summer ministering to a volleyball team instead of being in a discipleship group, but the commitment to do as the Lord directs is the key.

Ruth moved from a hedonistic society into a culture that attempted to please the God of the universe rather than the sensuous gods of the flesh. Within our advanced society of the 21st century, we often encounter women engaged in becoming part of self-serving singles' clubs, singles' dating services, singles' cruises, singles' meet markets...all created to keep singles busy in the waiting time of life. A committed single woman must be sensitive to the inevitable challenges she will meet in her attempt to live unselfishly in such a self-serving society.

One single was persecuted, not by non-Christians but by Christians, because she chose to spend her summer studying at a Bible institute rather than playing in the sunshine with her friends. They actually accused her of thinking she was better than them because she planned to study the Bible intensively for eight weeks. Unfortunately, our self-centered culture in the United States has penetrated the Church so much that a young woman not only has to choose against the American culture, but sometimes against the more subtle, worldly Christian subculture tainting the Body of Christ.

Ruth had to forsake the familiar and comfortable in order to receive God's best for her life.

Part of reckless abandonment is realizing how much our culture has affected our behavior patterns. You want to be Christlike, but your lifestyle is a reflection of *Vogue* magazine or *Cosmopolitan* rather than a new creation in Christ. A.W. Tozer said, "A whole new generation of Christians has come up believing that it is possible to 'accept' Christ without forsaking the world."[3] Ruth had to forsake the familiar and comfortable in order to receive God's best for her life.

New Faith

Ruth moved from a false religion into the only true and eternal relationship. Too many women have been involved in a form of religious worship, but have never had a vital, growing relationship with Jesus. Has your religious experience been like Isaiah 29:13b? *"Their worship of Me is made up only of rules taught by men"* (NIV). Has your faith been a lifeless ritual rather than a vital love relationship with Jesus? Why not spend some of your free hours as a single woman beginning a journey away from rituals into a deep relationship with Jesus Christ?

One single woman expressed this vital relationship with Jesus in the following way: "I desired that my relationship with the Lord be an adventure. One where I would find out what pleased Him and then do it, devoting as much energy to Jesus as I would in a relationship with a boyfriend. I am falling more in love with Jesus every day." Do you know more about pleasing a boyfriend than you do about pleasing the Lord Jesus?

Dividends from a High Price

Ruth's choice was costly, but the return on this high price far outweighed her investment. Matthew 19:29 says, *"And everyone who has left houses or brothers or sisters or father or mother or children or fields for My sake will receive a hundred times as much and will inherit eternal life"* (NIV). Ruth made the choice to turn her back on all that was familiar and begin a whole new life. Her "hundred times as much" was a godly husband, a son who would be the grandfather of King David, and inclusion in the lineage of Jesus Christ. She turned her back on all that was familiar, and God rewarded Ruth's critical choice.

Another costly aspect of Ruth's choice was the time frame in Israel's history. It was the age of the judges, a period of time described as "do your own thing"; *"Everyone did what was right in his own eyes"* (Judg. 21:25). Ruth chose not only to break her family cycle, but also to challenge the lifestyle that many in Israel embraced. She wanted God's will, not hers; His blueprints, not her elementary scribbling; God's assignment, not her foolish plans.

Whenever a single woman decides to abandon herself completely to Jesus, as Ruth did, she will find herself out of step with society and, sometimes, even with her friends. A single woman today needs the boldness to challenge and break the cycle of the "American way" that exalts a relationship with a man as the answer to life. This "American way" blurs the reality of the ultimate answer to life found in a deep relationship with Jesus Christ. A modern-day Ruth wrote, "My deep satisfaction from my commitment to Jesus is constantly challenged by other believers. They treat me like some kind of Neanderthal, definitely out of step with today's woman."

THE SHOUT-YES SINGLE

How does a woman display her own reckless abandon to God? Does she have to leave her family, hometown, and all her friends to prove such commitment?

Well, occasionally God might ask that of someone, but most of the time she simply needs to wake up in the morning and shout "Yes" to whatever the Lord has planned for her.

In his seminal work, *Mere Christianity*, C.S. Lewis described the opportunity we face every morning—and again and again throughout each day—to get to the yes:

> It comes the very moment you wake up each morning. All your wishes and hopes for the day rush at you like wild animals. And the *first* job each morning consists simply in shoving them all back; in listening to that other voice, taking that other point of view, letting that other larger, stronger, quieter life come flowing in. And so on, all day. Standing back from all your natural fussings and frettings; coming in out of the wind.

This shout-yes method may seem simplistic, but a teen girl who said yes to God was given the privilege of being the mother of Jesus, our Messiah. Mary was not chosen by God because she was superior to all the teen girls in her neighborhood or youth group. Mary was chosen because God knew she would say yes. Here is a teenager's response to the angel Gabriel:

> And Mary said, "Behold, the bondslave of the Lord; may it be done to me according to your word." And the angel departed from her (Luke 1:38).

In stark contrast to young Mary's yes to a Heaven-sent assignment, the Scripture tells us about an old priest who, six months earlier, struggled to say yes to his miracle when talking to that same angel Gabriel (see Luke 1). An adult who was a spiritual leader resisted the prospect of the miracle God was promising—a child given in old age. And here was the consummate irony: because of his struggle and hesitation to say the word *yes,* Zacharias (also known as *Zechariah*), the father of John the Baptist, was struck mute until his miracle son was born.

And behold, you shall be silent and unable to speak until the day when these things take place, because you did not believe my words... (Luke 1:20).

The angel Gabriel spoke with an old priest and a young girl, and the young girl responded with reckless abandon to a most amazing and challenging assignment. Saying yes to God is an act of daily surrender and a display of one's own reckless abandon.

DATELESS FRIDAY NIGHT MIRACLE (FROM *HOW TO AVOID A BOZO*)

Reckless abandon is a level of surrender that unlocks the greatest treasures God has in store for His kids. In fact, saying yes to Jesus has preceded every miracle I have ever experienced during the past forty-five years as His follower.

Sometimes we're challenged to say yes in some very interesting ways. My dating life altered pretty radically after I became a Christian, and let's just say, the guys weren't lining up at my door in college. But my girlfriends were—they were lining up to borrow my clothes for *their* dates! Saying yes to another outfit walking out my door on a dateless Friday night was a love response to Jesus and my sisters in Christ. It might seem like a small thing to someone, but I am well aware that I, like any girl, could have been petty or jealous; yet Jesus blessed that "practical faithfulness" in very special ways.

I always get a kick out of the fact that a friend actually got engaged in one of my favorite outfits. On their one-year anniversary, her husband asked if she could wear the cute outfit she wore the night they were engaged.

She laughed as she replied, "Sure! Let me call Jackie!"

He was taken aback. "Why on earth would you have to call Jackie?"

"Well, if I'm going to wear that dress, I need to borrow it, because that dress belongs to Jackie."

Ha! My clothes were very busy in college. Needless to say, I wasn't nearly as popular as my clothes that were always out on dates!

It was a regular thing that the gang I ran with would do something to entertain ourselves on the weekend; but on one of those dateless Friday nights (way back in 1972!), God gave me a holy nudge to stay back in my dorm instead of going to the mall with my friends. I said yes to time with Jesus in the Word—*yes* to a date night with Jesus.

As I was sitting in my room, my prayers went something like this: "Lord, I don't want to waste this time, and I don't want to feel sorry for myself. I need Your comfort. I need a word from You so I don't have to have these pity parties on Friday nights…Saturdays…Sunday afternoons—all the times I had assumed I would be dating!"

Although I was a young Christian, I knew the best thing to do when I wanted comfort is to open God's Word.

Although I was a young Christian, I *knew* the best thing to do when I wanted comfort. It wasn't to head to the mall, binge on cookie dough, or even call a friend. The best thing to do is to open God's Word. So in the dorm room on my date with Jesus, I decided to read the Book of Ruth. Just that morning, the chapel speaker had referred to that ancient text as a love story as well as the story of a young woman who broke her family's godless cycle and began a new life with the true God. In this precious little Book of Ruth, God showed me principles that became an outline for *How to Wait for God's Best*, the Bible study that led to *Lady In Waiting*; timeless concepts that are as relevant in the 21st century as they were in 1972…and in the ancient days of Ruth.

The miracle of finding these principles for avoiding a Bozo as a life-mate was not lost on me, because the miracle was (and is) *me!* My severely dysfunctional background had prepared me to pick a *loser*, quite frankly, even an abuser! Here is how my family is described on the back of my book, *Free Yourself to Love*.

As a survivor of severe childhood abuse, Jackie Kendall is an expert on forgiveness. A counselor deemed her family "one of the top-ten most dysfunctional in America." Though two siblings committed suicide and others adopted self-destructive lifestyles, Jackie wanted to break the mold and become a healthy, loving woman.

Given my upbringing, my family example, and the context of everybody I ran with, my lover was destined to be a Bozo. But God took that "given" and gave me something else in its place. He gave me an outline of His principles to protect me from settling for less than God's best! And then He gave me the privilege of sharing those principles with other single gals. And *then* He gave me my very own Boaz.

God exchanged my prospects for a Bozo with the gift of my Boaz.

On a dateless Friday night, I said yes to a holy nudge to spend extra time with Jesus, and I was spared the "living hell" of marrying a Bozo. Instead, I have been married to my Boaz for thirty-nine years. Through the message in the Book of Ruth, I learned how to break my family's destructive cycle and embrace, with reckless abandon, God's best for me.

THE MISSING PUZZLE PIECE

Often a woman will attempt to find delight in a career if Mr. Right has not arrived. In time, even her "great career" will prove to be less than satisfying. A career, a marriage, or even motherhood is not enough to totally satisfy you by itself. God knows that you will never be complete until you really understand that you are complete in Jesus. Colossians 2:9-10 says, *"For in Him all the fullness of Deity dwells in bodily form, and in Him you have been made complete, and He is the head over all rule and authority."* When a single woman enters a career or even marriage without understanding that she is complete in Christ, she will be disillusioned and dissatisfied.

God knows that you will never be complete until you really understand that you are complete in Jesus.

Incompleteness is not the result of being single, but of not being full of Jesus. Only in the process of reckless abandonment to Jesus does any woman ever finally understand that, in Him, she is complete. When two "incomplete" singles get married, their union will not make them complete. Their marriage will be simply two "incomplete" people trying to find completeness in one another. Only when they understand that their fullness is found in a relationship with Jesus will they ever begin to *complement* one another. They can never *complete* one another. You were not created to complete another, but to *complement*.

Completion is Jesus' responsibility and complementing is a woman's privilege. A woman not complete in Jesus will be a drain on her husband. Such a woman will expect her husband to fill the gap that only Jesus can fill. Only the single woman who understands this means of being complete in Jesus is mature enough to be a helpmeet (complement). *"For in Christ all the fullness of the Deity lives in bodily form, and you have been given fullness in Christ..."* (Col. 2:9-10 NIV). Are you feeling full yet? Ask the Lord right now to begin this process of revealing to your heart the reality of your fullness in Him. *"But it is good for me to draw near to God..."* (Ps. 73:28 KJV).

In the movie *Jerry Maguire*, the leading man played by Tom Cruise speaks a phrase that caused single women around the world to gasp for air! He said to his girlfriend, "You complete me!" Well, sorry girls, Jerry Maguire was *wrong*. It sounded good romantically, but biblically a woman was not created to *complete* a man but to *complement* a man (see Gen. 2:18).

In her book *Loneliness*, Elisabeth Elliot states, "Marriage teaches us that even the most intimate human companionship cannot satisfy the deepest places of the heart. Our hearts are lonely 'til they rest in Him."[4] Elisabeth Elliot has been married three times (twice widowed), and she knows from experience that marriage does not make one complete—only Jesus does.

SATISFIED BY A HEAVENLY FIANCÉ

Does your relationship with Jesus reflect reckless abandonment to Him, or does it reflect only tokenism, a superficial effort toward following Jesus? Are you content to offer to Jesus that which costs you nothing? Are you influencing those around you to consider a life-changing commitment to Jesus Christ? In the Song of Solomon, the Shulammite was so committed to the one she loved that other women wanted to meet him. They were anxious to go with her to seek him: *"Where has your lover gone, most beautiful of women? Which way did your lover turn, that we may look for him with you?"* (Song of Sol. 6:1 NIV). Who was this One so worthy of such reckless abandonment? Does your commitment to Jesus cause those around you to seriously consider whether Jesus is Lord of their lives? Or does your "token" relationship leave you and others still thirsty?

HONEYMOON WITH JESUS

One of Jackie's single friends stopped by her home one day, glowing and grinning from ear to ear. When questioned about her grin, she replied, "I am on a honeymoon with Jesus." This woman had been through a brutal divorce (including losing custody of her children), and in her hopeless condition she met the One who gives everlasting hope. When she began to recklessly abandon herself to knowing Jesus as Lord, He began to fill the gaps in her heart left by the removal of her husband and children. In Christ she found comfort, healing, direction, and purpose for her life.

Do you understand such a relationship with Christ? It doesn't come cheaply, but the high price is worth the results of such a commitment, especially today. The depth of your relationship with God is up to you. God has no favorites; the choice to surrender is yours. A.W. Tozer so brilliantly stated in his book *The Pursuit of God:* "It will require a determined heart and more than a little courage to wrench ourselves loose from the grip of our times and return to Biblical ways."[5]

Ruth had just such a determined heart, and the Lord honored her faith to move away from all that was familiar and take a journey toward the completely unknown. Ruth did not allow her friends, her old surroundings, or her culture's dead faith to keep her from running hard after God. She did not use the excuse of a dark past to keep her from a bright future that began with her first critical choice: reckless abandonment to Jesus Christ.

Have you made this critical choice or you have settled for a mediocre relationship with Jesus? Amy Carmichael, one of the greatest single woman missionaries who ever lived, once remarked, "The saddest thing one meets is the nominal Christian."[6]

Choose right now to put mediocrity behind you; courageously determine to pursue Jesus with your whole heart, soul, and mind.

Choose right now to put mediocrity behind you; courageously determine to pursue Jesus with your whole heart, soul, and mind. As a single woman, this is the perfect moment to establish a radical relationship with Jesus and remove any tokenism from your Christian walk.

Becoming a Lady in Waiting begins with reckless abandonment to Jesus. The strength and discipline necessary to be a Lady of Diligence, Faith, Virtue, Devotion, Purity, Security, Contentment, Conviction, and Patience is discovered in this radical way of relating to your heavenly Bridegroom. If you find yourself struggling with any of the qualities discussed in the following chapters, you may want to reexamine your own commitment to Jesus. Is it real and all-encompassing, or merely ornamental? Do you remember a time when you broke your "alabaster box" in the presence of the Lord Jesus? The Lady in Waiting understands the pleasing aroma of the perfume that flows from one's "broken alabaster box." It is the irresistible aroma of reckless abandonment to Jesus Christ.

BECOMING A LADY OF RECKLESS ABANDONMENT

- From your perspective, what is the difference between "token commitment" and "reckless abandonment" to Jesus? Is your relationship with Jesus one of sacrifice or convenience? (See Second Samuel 24:24.)

- Have you broken your "alabaster box" at the feet of Jesus? (See Mark 14:3-9 and Luke 7:36-39.) Are you afraid to break your box at His feet? Why?

- Like Ruth, how has your relationship with Jesus affected your friends, your surroundings, and your faith? (See Matthew 19:29.)

- Does your life have public and private evidences of your reckless abandonment to Jesus Christ? Explain.

- Read Colossians 2:10. What does being complete in Jesus mean to you? In what ways do you feel incomplete? How can that be changed?

- Have you experienced the completeness that comes from the courtship available with your heavenly Fiancé? Consider this dating prerequisite: You must understand you are complete in Jesus before you ever date or marry.

- What does the following statement mean to you: "Any woman who does not understand that she is complete in Jesus is susceptible to idolatry"? (This idolatry is dependence on a guy to make her complete—thus putting him in God's place.) Consider this verse: "*How happy are those who know their need for God...*" (Matt. 5:3 PNT).

ENDNOTES

1. Kenneth G. Smith, *Learning to Be a Woman* (Downers Grove, IL: InterVarsity Press, 1970), back cover.

2. Scofield Bible (New York, NY: Oxford University Press, 1967), 51, note on Genesis 35:19.

3. A.W. Tozer, *The Pursuit of God* (Camp Hill, PA: Christian Publications, 1982), 16.

4. Elisabeth Elliot, *Loneliness* (Nashville, TN: Oliver Nelson, 1988), 16.

5. Tozer, *The Pursuit of God*, 29.

6. Quoted in Elisabeth Elliot, *A Chance to Die* (Old Tappan, NJ: Fleming H. Revell Company, 1987), 117.

Chapter 2

LADY OF DILIGENCE

Through all her activities, the Lady of Diligence can have a ministry of encouragement—to give someone who is discouraged the will to continue and a reason to keep going! –JMK

While getting ready for a speaking engagement, she managed to get the kids up, dressed, and fed; fill the lunch boxes; load everyone in the car; and take them to school. Then she hurried home to set her hair and do her makeup. Finally dressed and ready to go speak, she made one last dash for the bathroom. While washing her hands, she noticed that the toilet was overflowing—not a slow drip, but pouring out all over the floor and into her open-toed shoes and nylons. She scrambled for towels and used them to build a dike then rubbed her feet dry and squirted her shoes with perfume. She ran out the door and jumped into the car. Halfway to the church she realized that she had left her Bible and outlines on the kitchen counter.

Such is the drama of Jackie Kendall's daily life. This kind of insanity is not unique to her. Every wife and mother daily deal with the legitimate needs of her husband and children. These needs take precedence over anything she might want to do, regardless of how "noble" her desires are! To be involved in the simplest form of ministry may require the married woman three times as much time to accomplish, compared to the single woman. Although a single woman may long for the "chaos" of a family, she must not waste her time wishing for it. She must be diligent to use her single time wisely now. She has more control over her time and choices now than she will probably ever have again. (The single parent is not included in this comparison because her responsibilities are double that of a married woman. She must go "solo" in raising children, increasing the burden of her daily priorities even more.)

The perfect time to make the most of every opportunity is while you are single. Every believer should use time wisely, as Ephesians 5:15-17 (NIV) says:

Be very careful, then, how you live—not as unwise but as wise, making the most of every opportunity, because the days are evil. Therefore do not be foolish, but understand what the Lord's will is.

John Fischer wrote this:

God has called me to live now. He wants me to realize my full potential as a man right now, to be thankful about where I am, and to enjoy it to the fullest. I have a strange feeling that the single person who is always wishing he were married will probably get married, discover all that is involved, and wish he were single again! He will ask himself, "Why didn't I use that time for the Lord when I didn't have so many other obligations? Why didn't I give myself totally to Him when I was single?"[1]

The single woman can be involved in the Lord's work on a level that a married woman cannot because of the distractions and responsibilities of being a wife and mother. Ironically, some single women can be so distressed by their single state that they become emotionally more distracted than a wife and mother of four children.

Ironically, some single women can be so distressed by their single state that they become emotionally more distracted than a wife and mother of four children.

Rather than staying home worrying about another "dateless" Saturday night, realize how much valuable time has been entrusted to you at this point in your life. Rather than resent your many single hours, embrace them as a gift from God—a package that contains opportunities to serve Him that are limited only by your own self-pity and lack of obedience.

No Time to Waste

Understanding God's promised provision for widows, Naomi sent Ruth to gather grain in the field of a kinsman. Ruth was willing to use her life working diligently at whatever her Lord called her to do. She would not be paralyzed by her lack of a husband:

And Ruth the Moabitess said to Naomi, "Please let me go to the field and glean among the ears of grain after one in whose sight I may find favor." And she said to her, "Go, my daughter" (Ruth 2:2).

Ruth also did not allow the fact that she was a stranger from Moab to cause her to fear while she was gleaning in a stranger's field. Ruth was the "new girl in town," an obvious newcomer, but she was not afraid to walk into a totally unfamiliar situation. Countless single women stay home rather than travel alone into the unknown. They not only miss out on being encouraged by others, but also are not exposed to new relationships when they remain at home tied up by cords of fear and feeling sorry for themselves.

If a single woman allows the fearful prospect of meeting new people and new challenges to keep her at home, she may find herself bored and lonely while all the time missing many satisfying and fulfilling experiences. Don't stay home as a fearful single woman. Take that step of faith and volunteer. Get involved and see what you have been missing. One single said, "Serving the Lord brings such inexpressible joy." People who are not involved in serving the Lord obviously have never experienced this joy; otherwise, churches wouldn't have to beg them to get involved. If all the singles in the church just realized their "strategic position," churches would never need to ask for help with children, youth, or college students. There would probably be so many available single workers that there would be a "surplus of manpower"!

FREE TO FOLLOW

Are you busy serving Jesus during your free time, or do you waste hours trying to pursue and snag an available guy? Ruth was a widow, but she did not use her time sponsoring pity parties for all unhappy single women to gather and compare the misery of datelessness. When she and Naomi moved back to Bethlehem, Ruth did not waste a moment feeling sorry for herself. She went right to work. Instead of being drained by her discouraging circumstances, she took advantage of them and diligently embraced each day.

Ruth came to the God of Israel after years of living in darkness, and He gladly received her service even though she was a Moabite foreigner. She bound herself to the service of the Lord, interweaving her service with Him like the braiding of a heavy rope. Isaiah 56:6-7 (NIV) refers to a foreigner binding himself (or herself) to the Lord and Him willingly receiving their "diligent" service: *"And foreigners who bind themselves to the Lord to serve Him…these I will bring to My holy mountain…"*

Are you tightly bound to the Lord, serving Him diligently, or has your relationship and service been unraveling over the years as you continue to be single and not married? Has resentment and self-pity unraveled what used to be a tightly woven labor for the Lord? You must be sensitive to the things and situations that distract you from redeeming your free time:

> Whatever might blur the vision God had given [Amy Carmichael] of His work, whatever could distract or deceive or tempt others to seek anything but the Lord Jesus Himself she tried to eliminate.[2]

Some singles see the lack of a mate as God denying them something for a more "noble purpose"—*a cross to bear!* Our selfish nature tends to focus on what we do not have rather than on what we do have—free time—that can be used for others and ourselves. Is your life on hold until you have someone to hold?

Sitting in a restaurant across from a beautiful blonde, as the woman's personal story began to unfold, the listener was somewhat overwhelmed. Here was a very attractive woman who had put her life with Jesus on hold after her world fell apart. She had been married for a few years and was trying to conceive a child, when she heard her single best friend was pregnant. What irony: her unmarried friend was with child, and she remained childless. The irony turned into a trauma when this married woman found out that the father was her own husband. Can you imagine the devastation caused in this beautiful young woman's heart? Have you experienced such a crushing emotional blow?

The stunned listener began to cry out for wisdom concerning this tragedy. Jesus reminded the listener that God is not intimidated by trauma. In fact, Psalm 34:18 says, *"The Lord is near to the brokenhearted and saves those who are crushed in spirit."* This brokenhearted woman had put her life on hold after her husband divorced her. Such a response is understandable, but that day in the restaurant this now single woman decided to take her broken heart, her empty arms, and her loneliness and give them to Jesus. In exchange, Jesus taught her how to resist feeling sorry for herself and how to stop living in the arena of bitterness.

After she made the choice of recklessly abandoning herself to Jesus as Lord, she was free to serve Him. This once brokenhearted single woman has been transformed into a fearless servant of the Lord. In fact, she became a missionary to Quito, Ecuador.

Have you also put your life on hold? Do you have an excuse for not serving Jesus?

A FULL PLACE SETTING

A former college friend remained single longer than any of us ever expected. She had dated incessantly in college, so we assumed if any of the girls would marry, it would be Donna. Ten years after her graduation from college, she was not married. Someone asked what helped her to be so satisfied as a single woman. Her immediate response was, "A full place setting."

She had lived for several years eating her meals on paper plates while her good china and flatware were snugly stored in her hope chest. Then the Lord showed her that she did not have to wait for a "mate" to bring beauty to her private world. She unpacked her china and silver and began not only to entertain others in style, but also to daily set out china and crystal for herself.

(One Wednesday night at church, Donna sat in front of two people who were to become her future in-laws. They did not know each other at the time. On the way home from church, the future father-in-law remarked that he thought Donna would become his daughter-in-law. He was absolutely right. This satisfied single woman has someone sharing her china and crystal today, but her feelings of satisfaction did not come because of a husband. She found satisfaction by serving the Lord.)

**Life is satisfying only when you diligently
serve the Lord, whatever your circumstances.**

Some women put their lives on hold, each waiting for some guy to come riding into her life on a white stallion. They have no china, no decent furniture, and no pictures on the walls—none of the little extras that make a house inviting. They make minimal investment in what they hope is a temporary condition. Their lives reflect a "paper plate" mentality. They cannot comprehend fullness and satisfaction without a man. These precious women have settled for the "generic" version of life. How unlike Jesus' statement in John 10:10, in which He said He came so we might have a more abundant life. Do you believe that the abundant life is only for the married woman? Do you think that a woman with a husband, two children, a nice home, and two insurance policies is more satisfied with life than you are? Life is satisfying only when you diligently serve the Lord, whatever your circumstances.

ENVIABLE SINGLENESS

Singleness is an enviable condition. An unmarried woman has something that a married woman gives up on her wedding day: extra time for Jesus. Too many young women waste valuable years as they wait for life to begin—after marriage. They rarely realize the priceless free time they waste, until it is gone. Have you neglected some mission or ministry opportunities because you feared prolonging your unmarried state?

A young woman heard about this enviable condition and wrote a letter asking Jackie whether she should pursue a doctorate degree. (She continues to count more birthdays as a single than she had anticipated.) Jackie enthusiastically encouraged her to immediately get her degree. As a single woman, she diligently hit the books without neglecting a mate or a child. Her single state served as the perfect qualification for the pursuit of a doctorate. This is not to say that a woman can't pursue her dreams after she is married, but she will have a much higher price to pay and often the pursued dream turns into a nightmare!

If you love serving Jesus, please do not waste any of the free time you have. Do not consider yourself too unhappy to help anyone else. Self-centeredness will rob you of the joy of serving. Satan, who is effective at distracting you from God's best, wants you to continue dreaming about how "one day" you will get involved in ministry. He wants to sidetrack you from making a lasting investment. Too many women foolishly believe his lies. Therefore, they lose sight of opportunities to get involved in any form of outreach to others. Unsatisfied and unfulfilled, they sink deep into the quicksand of "maybe next year."

Many have embraced the ultimate deception, "poor me." An excerpt from a single friend's letter exposes this self-pitying lie: "As is usually the case, as soon as I stopped asking what was in it for me and began asking what I was meant to give, things began to improve, beginning with my attitude. I continue to grow and be greatly strengthened in my relationship with God one on one and to seek out where I can serve those around me." This single woman is a classic beauty. She has learned how to use her free time for Jesus rather than sit home writing melancholy poetry.

"SPOILED KATHY EDWARDS"

At least twice a month I receive an e-mail from one struggling single girl or another. As I read the details of their prolonged singleness and the discontentment that almost always follows, I can't help but think of another single woman I have nicknamed "Spoiled K.E."

Before you jump to conclusions, K.E. isn't a spoiled brat! She isn't spoiled rotten, and she isn't a spoil sport. No! This single woman has faced prolonged singleness and has not wasted an ounce of it in discontentment. Instead she has lived a life of reckless abandon to Jesus, and she is one of the most *blessed* women I have ever known. She uses her free time wisely, serving every chance she gets. She encourages other single women not to settle for Bozo guys. She travels all across the United States as a traveling nurse, and everywhere she lands, she makes Jesus look stunning. I have watched God bless this single woman for the past fifteen years, answering her prayers and her heart's cry so regularly that I've come to consider her "spoiled" by God. When I came across this verse the other day, Spoiled K.E. came to my mind:

> *How great is the goodness You have stored up for those who fear* [honor] *you. You lavish it on those who come to you for protection, blessing them before the watching world* (Psalm 31:19 NLT).

Kathy Edwards is so busy being a blessing and so consumed with honoring *the Lord,* that she is constantly experiencing God's "stored up blessings" with her name on them. It has been a joy to watch the Lord bless her all these years. May her tribe increase!

UNRELENTING PURSUIT

Undistracted and unrelenting describe different facets of the word *diligence.* The Lady of Diligence embodies these terms. A verse that describes her attitude toward ministry and service is First Corinthians 15:58 (NIV): *"Therefore, my dear brothers, stand firm. Let nothing move you. Always give yourselves fully to the work of the Lord, because you know that your labor in the Lord is not in vain."* Do these terms describe your attitude and approach to using your free time for Jesus? Let's examine how diligence affects every aspect of your service and ministry for the Lord.

DILIGENCE AND THE MINISTRY OF TEACHING

Have you been diligently pursuing truth for years, but not giving out as much as you have taken in? Are you involved in a regular Bible study where you give, maybe even teach? Almost as dangerous as neglecting the Word is the habit of taking it in but not putting it into practice. "Impression without expression can lead to depression." Do you keep attending church, Sunday school, Bible studies, seminars, and retreats—taking yet never giving?

Almost as dangerous as neglecting the Word is the habit of taking it in but not putting it into practice. "Impression without expression can lead to depression."

Take advantage of this time in your life when you can be involved in teaching without so many encumbrances. Maybe you've considered leading a discipleship group. Hesitate no more; go for it! There is no time in your life more perfect than now. Maybe you have toyed with the idea of teaching a Bible study. Do not delay. The future may hold more distractions that would continue to keep you from your goal.

DILIGENCE AND THE MINISTRY OF ENCOURAGEMENT

How many times a week do you find yourself in a position where someone has shared a need with you and you want so much to respond with wisdom and grace? Isaiah 50:4 (NIV) says:

> *The Sovereign Lord has given me an instructed tongue, to know the word that sustains the weary. He wakens me morning by morning, wakens my ear to listen like one being taught.*

Do you have a hard time responding to such an early morning wake-up call? Rising early to develop the tongue of a disciple will open a door of ministry to those who are weary, whether they are at work, at church, or even at the grocery store. Your very words will be a ministry of healing and encouragement. *"The tongue that brings healing is a tree of life, but a deceitful tongue crushes the spirit"* (Prov. 15:4 NIV). Such predawn training will give you the privilege of becoming God's garden hose in a land of many thirsty people.

DILIGENCE AND THE MINISTRY OF PRAYER

I once heard someone describe prayer as internal jogging. For those of us who have jogged or run (or in my case, done years of speed-walking), we know that to build up endurance and ability is a process. As with physical exercise, the only way to fail at prayer is to fail to show up.

Prayer is communication between two people who love each other. When life is difficult, these trials are perfect material for prayer: fears, shattered dreams, broken engagements, difficulties in a friend's family…all the high-anxiety situations in life!

Do you have a prayer partner? Or do you only have someone with whom you have regular pity parties? If you do not have a prayer partner, ask the Lord right now for such a gift. A prayer partner can help you pray for others. Of course, this prayer partner needs to be a female, one who can encourage you to keep God's perspective on your commitment to being all God wants you to be, whether married or single.

"A prayer partnership serves as one of the greatest assets for accomplishing the deepest and highest work of the human spirit: prayer."[3] Praying regularly with someone (or a small group) is such a vital part of your service to God. To intercede on behalf of someone else's need is a privilege. When you intercede with a partner, the "duet" of harmony before God can change your world. Matthew 18:19 (NIV) describes this harmonious duet: *"Again, I tell you that if two of you on earth agree about anything you ask for, it will be done for you by My Father in heaven."* That little verb *agree* refers to harmony. Do you have someone with whom you can prayerfully approach God in harmony? Rather than searching for a life partner, look for a prayer partner. Together you can participate in God-given prayer projects. Together you can discover how you can take your concerns for others and turn them into prayer projects.

DILIGENCE AND THE MINISTRY OF SERVICE

It is doubtful that there could ever be a better time to serve Jesus than this "moment" of singleness. Rather than wasting precious moments fantasizing about an earthly lover, take advantage of your free hours each day to serve the Lord of Heaven. If you are frustrated and distracted rather than fruitfully serving Jesus, then ask Him right now to adjust your vision.

As Ruth diligently worked at what she could, God sent her a man to protect and provide for her. God will do the same for you if that is His plan. Is there a ministry opportunity you should be working with? Why not consider a short-term mission trip?

Don't worry about that certain guy you have had your eye on for a while. If he is God's best for you, he will be there when you return. Your single state may not be permanent, but it definitely is not to be a comatose state until your Prince Charming arrives and whisks you off to his castle. Single women are not "Sleeping Beauties" waiting for their prince to fight his way through the thorns and past the wicked witch to finally kiss them awake. That is an illusion often used by the enemy to defraud women.

Is there an opportunity of service that you have avoided because you can't give up your "post on the castle wall" looking for your knight in shining armor? Is there an application for a summer ministry waiting for you to fill out? Such a chance may come again next summer, but then it will be even harder to respond to the prospect of serving, for time brings more and more distractions. As you get older, you assume more obligations and responsibilities that demand your time and attention. Such distractions will make serving Jesus even more difficult. Have you given Jesus full reign over your time?

**Don't waste your singleness! This is the time to develop
an eternal skill set that will not only bless your singleness
but also your marriage and parenting some day!**

I have noticed that single women who have learned how to serve effectively during their free hours are the very women who, when married, can squeeze into their crazy-paced life chances to serve. Those singles who didn't use their free time for Jesus are more likely to pass up a chance to serve Jesus when they are busy as married women. Don't waste your singleness! This is the time to develop an eternal skill set that will not only bless your singleness but also your marriage and parenting some day!

Limitless ministry opportunities exist for the Lady of Diligence. These ministries are available right this moment. They do not demand a Bible college education. The only requirement is a single woman who desires to use her time wisely in ministry.

DILIGENCE AND THE MINISTRY OF WRITING

This ministry requires pen, paper, and a willing heart. Much of the New Testament was originally written as letters to believers. An encouraging letter or postcard can be read and re-read. So often a person will think about writing someone a letter, but the thought never becomes action. You may ignore the inward suggestion because of a busy schedule or a resistance to writing. A personal note, though, serves as oxygen to the soul of the recipient. *"He who refreshes others will himself be refreshed"* (Prov. 11:25 NIV).

With the cost of greeting cards increasing to the price of what used to be the cost of a book, I may not send actual cards as frequently as I used to, but there are plenty of other methods to communicate words of hope, including e-mail messages, texting, and even phone calls.

Whether the encouragement is spoken or written, the ministry of encouragement is a critical part of soul care.

If you are not comfortable writing a full letter, or your schedule does not permit such a ministry in writing, then purchase some pre-stamped postcards and try to send them regularly to different people who need a refreshing word. Write an e-mail or send a Facebook message. The Lord wants you to be involved in the lives of those around you, and writing is one of those opportunities.

DILIGENCE AND THE MINISTRY OF LISTENING

A ministry of listening is available right now. When someone is grieving, your presence provides more power than words. When someone is burdened, you may want to just listen and silently pray rather than verbally give the solution to the problem. Being content to listen to someone today is a gift you can give. A listener provides a healing audience for someone who is hurting. When Jackie's sister died, listeners who allowed her to share the loss and cry freely were God's greatest source of comfort. Being content to listen is a gift you can give to someone today.

It may take a gentle touch to minister to the spirit. It also may require just being with the person, whether standing for hours in a hospital hallway or sitting by a sickbed. Sometimes even the greatest songs or truths are not the appropriate thing during a crisis: *"Like one who takes away a garment on a cold day, or like vinegar poured on soda, is one who sings songs to a heavy heart"* (Prov. 25:20 NIV). This ministry requires not seminary training, but a loving, listening heart.

Listening to a person is like being a bucket for the heart's well. Most women need to talk to think. Wise is the woman who not only knows how to listen but also knows how to ask key questions. This listening and asking questions is a profound ministry. Proverbs clearly states the effectiveness of "a bucket" used to draw up purpose and understanding from someone's heart,

"The purposes of a man's heart are deep waters, but a man of understanding draws them out" (Proverbs 20:5 NIV).

DILIGENCE AND THE MINISTRY OF HOSPITALITY

The ministry of hospitality doesn't require a meal worthy of Martha Stewart or your home fit for HGTV. It is simply cooking for others as a significant ministry, especially during illness or bereavement. Casseroles and cakes can be such a blessing to a new mother, an elderly neighbor, or someone emotionally devastated by a death in the family. What a way to share the love of Christ with someone who needs to see Christianity in action.

Please do not limit your ministry of hospitality to candlelight dinners for the man of your dreams. Think how a beautiful, candlelight dinner for a group of single women, or even high school girls, could minister to them.

DILIGENCE AND THE MINISTRY OF HELPS

This ministry requires time, but it is invaluable. Helping others with the "dailies" of life is a gift that breaks their exhausting monotony. Helping a friend get her apartment ready for special guests, or helping her move into a new place, leaves the recipient grateful. Mere physical labor may seem so insignificant in comparison to church visitation, but the Word of God speaks clearly to such a misconception. *"Whether, then, you eat or drink or whatever you do, do all to the glory of God"* (1 Cor. 10:31). Maybe a friend needs a ride to the airport during rush hour, or maybe she needs her oven cleaned, or even her laundry done. These duties can all be done unto the Lord. *"Whatever you do, work at it with all your heart, as working for the Lord, not for men"* (Col. 3:23 NIV).

NON-NEWSY WORKS

For those of you who are diligently going after Jesus and the privilege of serving Him, here is a very special reminder. Sometimes you will be called to do some monotonous work that will not make the headlines. It may frustrate you because it doesn't seem very "impressive." Consider the reality of all the non-newsy things Jesus did during the majority of His life (thirty years), before He began His formal ministry. What more humbling work could Ruth have done than gathering leftover grain for the survival of her mother-in-law and herself?

I read a comment in the best-selling book *Kisses from Katie* that addresses brilliantly what I have observed. I imagine the author would have admired

Ruth's diligence and her willingness to do something so humbling. Here is what Katie said:

> People who really want to make a difference in the world usually do it, in one way or another. And I've noticed something about people who make a difference in the world: They hold the unshakable conviction that individuals are extremely important, that *every life matters*. They get excited over one smile. They are willing to feed one stomach, educate one mind, and treat one wound. They aren't determined to revolutionize the world all at once; they're satisfied with small changes. Over time, though, the small changes add up. Sometimes they even transform cities and nations, and yes, the world.[4]

Becoming a Lady of Diligence happens one small change at a time, not all at once! And sometimes it happens from the outside in. Sometimes we have to *do* the thing to *become* the thing.

Sometimes we have to do the thing to become the thing.

Richard Foster brilliantly penned this thought, "If all of our serving is before others, we will be shallow people indeed."[5] Jesus spoke clearly about the constant public display of our service. *"Everything they do is done for men to see..."* (Matt. 23:5 NIV). The next time someone asks you to help out in service that is monotonous and non-newsy, don't hesitate. The King records such works (see Matt. 25:34-35). Teaching Bible studies, going out on evangelism teams, mission trips, and even prayer groups—all these are priceless opportunities to serve, but they are not the only avenues. Serving in the preschool department at church, going to kids' camp, and even cooking in the kitchen for a junior high banquet are all honorable services that the Lady of Diligence can embrace with respect.

Look at your schedule and decide how some of your free time that was wasted yesterday might be redeemed today. Allow no more room in your schedule for "pity parties." Such wise use of your free time will give you the gift of "no regrets." Your future service will be focused and no longer distracted.

Free hours,
Not wasted by me,
Using my free time,
To serve only Thee.
Realizing how temporary free time will be
Never to regret a missed opportunity,
For others to be blest,
Through yielded me. —JMK

BECOMING A LADY OF DILIGENCE

- Determine what may have kept you from being more involved in ministry by seeing which of the following four characters you identify with the most.

1. Jealous Jenny: Do you focus on the gifts others have been given and, therefore, never find your own niche in ministry? Have you unwisely compared yourself with other women? (See First Corinthians 4:7; 12:7; Romans 12:3.)

2. Diva Danielle: Do you want to serve God on your terms? Do you want to write the script and have the leading role? (See John 4:34; 7:16,18; Matthew 23:5.)

3. Fearful Fiona: Do you fear what others think? Are you afraid of becoming too involved and being labeled a fanatic? Do you hesitate to be a Lady of Diligence because you feel so inadequate? (See Proverbs 29:25; Second Timothy 1:7; First Thessalonians 5:24.)

4. Doubting Debby: Faith is believing what God says about you. Do you long to become more involved in a number of ministries, but feel your faith will fizzle before you finish? Have you struggled with serving the Lord in the past, so you doubt yourself today? (Part of ministry is learning, so don't let yesterday's struggles prevent future successes.) (See First John 4:4; Second Timothy 1:9; First Timothy 6:12.)

- To get involved in any ministry demands a sacrifice. Have you allowed your self-centeredness to dominate your daily schedule? Why not go through your checkbook tonight and see how many checks were written for things concerning others? (See Second Samuel 24:24; Philippians 2:3-4; Matthew 19:29.)

- Discuss the following quote from *Kisses from Katie* and compare it to the Scriptures cited: "People who really want to make a difference in the world usually do it, in one way or another. And I've noticed something about people who make a difference in the world: They hold the unshakable conviction that individuals are extremely important, that *every life matters.* They get excited over one smile. They are willing to feed one stomach, educate one mind, and treat one wound. They aren't determined to revolutionize the world all at once; they're satisfied with small changes. Over time, though, the small changes add up. Sometimes they even transform cities and nations, and yes, the world." (See Colossians 3:23-24; First Corinthians 10:31.)

ENDNOTES

1. John Fischer, *A Single Person's Identity* (Discovery Papers, Catalog No. 3154, August 5, 1973), 3.

2. Elisabeth Elliot, *A Chance to Die* (Old Tappan, NJ: Fleming H. Revell Company, 1987), 117.

3. Charles F. Stanley, *Handle With Prayer* (Wheaton, IL: Victory Books, 1982), 15.

4. Katie Davis, *Kisses from Katie* (Nashville, TN: Howard Books, 2012), 11.

5. Richard J. Foster, *Celebration of Discipline* (San Francisco, CA: Harper & Row Publishers, 1978), 117.

Chapter 3

LADY OF FAITH

*There is no success, no happiness, and no fulfillment in life
apart from a consistent, daily, growing relationship
with Jesus through the Word.* –M.E. Cravens

If you are spouse-hunting, we have heard that Alaska, South Dakota, and Utah have an abundance of men. Proportionately, women most outnumber men in the Northeastern states. Are you panicked because you are residing in one of these male-sparse states? Do you suddenly have the urge to relocate? Don't start packing yet!

I came across a survey done by "The Oprah Show" and *Men's Health* magazine that lists the top 20 cities to meet single men who are over 35. Here's the criteria they looked at, according to David Zinczenko, the magazine's editor in chief—"the ratio of unmarried men to unmarried women, divorce rates, fitness level, philanthropy, education level and attraction." Says Zinczenko, "We crunched the numbers every which way—up and down, all around, and tried to find the best way to up your chances of finding men who are single, straight, smart, who are emotionally available."

Did your city make the top 20?

1. San Jose, California

2. Salt Lake City, Utah

3. Arlington, Texas

4. Raleigh, North Carolina

5. San Francisco, California

6. Fremont, California

7. Austin, Texas

8. Minneapolis, Minnesota

9. Washington, DC

10. San Diego, California

11. Charlotte, North Carolina

12. Dallas, Texas

13. Denver, Colorado

14. St. Paul, Minnesota

15. Seattle, Washington

16. Houston, Texas

17. New York, New York

18. Madison, Wisconsin

19. Fort Worth, Texas

20. Durham, North Carolina[1]

The Census Bureau in 2010 confirmed the US female population being higher than males—with the exception of ten states, including Alaska, Wyoming, and Hawaii. However, an article in *USA Today* stated: "The Census Bureau reports today that for the first time since the early 1900s, the USA's male population grew faster than the female in the 1980s."[2] Are you breathing easier? Such a statistic does not alleviate your need to be a Lady of Faith. The existence of more single men does not mean exemption from the often trying process of waiting for God's best by faith.

ENROLLED TO GET YOUR MRS. DEGREE

One friend assumed that by going to a big Christian college, she would inevitably find Mr. Right. Considering that she was from a very small town where more livestock lived than people, her strategy for finding a spouse seemed quite logical. She completed her four years and returned home without her "MRS." degree. Where do you think she found her mate? You guessed it, back in her very small hometown.

Her father invited her to come and watch their church baseball team, and guess who showed up on the opposing team? Mr. Right, a guy she had met at youth camp more than a decade earlier. You know the rest of the story. Her logic did not find Mr. Right. She returned to a hometown barren of many males, and God, who is not limited by our circumstances, delivered her mate from way out in "left field." God did not honor her logic, but He did honor her faith in Him to meet her needs.

God delivered her mate from way out in "left field." God did not honor her logic, but He did honor her faith in Him to meet her needs.

Do you presently live in a town or city where you need "eyes of faith" in relation to the prospects of a mate? Do you attend a church where the "pickins are slim"? Let's take a closer look at two contrasting attitudes toward a person's circumstances.

Where the Boys Are

Think back to how the love story in the Book of Ruth began. Three widows, Naomi with her two daughters-in-law, Orpah and Ruth, have just been through the painful experience of losing the men they loved. Just facing each day without their mates required much faith because of the difficulty in providing for one's own needs. Naomi, being a Jewess, made the decision to leave Moab and return to her hometown in Israel (Bethlehem). Her two daughters-in-law had become young widows, so she encouraged them to return to their families where they each might find another husband. Naomi's suggestion appeared very rational. Naomi knew that they (being Moabites) had a better chance of finding husbands in Moab than in Israel.

> *...Go back, each of you, to your mother's home. May the Lord show kindness to you, as you have shown to your dead and to me. May the Lord grant that each of you will find rest in the home of another husband* (Ruth 1:8-9 NIV).

Would Ruth have ever found a godly husband to be united with if she had also returned to Moab?

Naomi lovingly pointed Orpah and Ruth in the direction of possible prospects. She actually encouraged them to go in a direction where they could *see* how they might each find a husband. Orpah followed Naomi's advice and chose logical sight for future direction. She gave Naomi a kiss good-bye and headed "where the boys are." Such "choices" are often based on logical sight and do not need even a mustard seed of faith.

Many single women spend their free time searching for the same kind of location chosen by Orpah. They attend schools because they can "see" the prospects. They join churches based on apparent ratios of men to women. They go to seminars, retreats, and conferences looking for the man of their dreams, only to demand a refund for the nightmare they often find (the ratio of women to men typically registered at retreats being seven women to every one man).

Some women have changed churches because they were in a "no prospective mate" district. Others avoid churches under-stocked with available men. Can you relate? Some single women serve only one term on a mission field and never return because the ratio of available men to women shrinks even smaller on the mission field than in their home church. A single woman serving as a missionary wrote: "Well, here I am in a no-hope situation. There is only one single man to about fifty single women." On what are these women focusing—on the situation or on the Sovereign One?

CHANCE RENDEZVOUS

A woman who takes the route of Orpah (sensual, logical sight) often invents ways for a "chance rendezvous" with the man of her dreams. You can see her loitering in the very area that Mr. Right regularly frequents, hoping that he might finally notice her and the romance will begin. This sounds more like a Harlequin romance. Such a young woman might sing in the choir, not because she wants to make a joyful noise unto the Lord, but because she wants a weekly chance to sit near the prospect (single man) that her "sensual sight" has focused upon. Such impure motives for such a noble cause! Proverbs 19:14 says, *"House and wealth are an inheritance from fathers, but a prudent wife is from the Lord."*

If the Lord wants to give you a man, He does not need your clever "chance rendezvous." This is not advocating that you avoid men completely and expect the Lord to "UPS" His choice to your front door. You need to participate in activities that involve men and women, but be sensitive to your motives whenever you find yourself in the presence of "available men." Consider this Scripture whenever checking your motives and your pulse! Proverbs 16:2 (NIV) says, *"All a man's ways seem innocent to him, but motives are weighed by the Lord."*

"All a man's ways seem innocent to him, but motives are weighed by the Lord."

You can prevent disappointing moments if you check your heart whenever you go to a singles' activity. Much preparation (like taking a shower, putting on makeup, styling your hair, doing your nails, and choosing the perfect outfit) precedes one's attending such an activity, yet so little heart preparation does. The gal with sensual sight can become so obsessed with finding her guy that she neglects her inner self. Orpah's style (logical sight) tends to become the norm, but Ruth offers an alternative to this vain search for Mr. Right. She demonstrates what it means to be a Lady of Faith.

EYES OF FAITH

Orpah's example of going after the available men could have influenced Ruth to return to Moab, the home of her parents and the gods of her youth. Ruth, however, remained with Naomi and her God. Ruth certainly must have considered the probability of remaining single if she went with Naomi. Even though it promised no prospects of a husband, she chose to follow Naomi and her God back to Bethlehem. Ruth chose to trust God with her future. She looked not with sensual sight, but through "eyes of faith." Even though Ruth was young in her faith in the God of Israel, she chose to trust with her heart for the future her eyes could not yet see.

The International Children's Bible describes faith in this way: *"Faith means being sure of the things we hope for. And faith means knowing that something is real even if we do not see it"* (Heb. 11:1). This childlike expression of such an abstract quality can become a daily reality in the life of the Lady of Faith. Your hope cannot be put in some dreamed-up future. It must be in the God who knows your past, present, and future, and loves you enough to give you the best.

NO-HOPE SITUATION

Are you in what seems like a "no-hope situation"? Maybe you are attending a church that requires you to exercise faith to even open the door and go in, since every man there is either married, engaged, or the age of your baby brother. Instead of becoming fearful during this trying situation, look to the Lord through eyes of faith. To do so brings God great pleasure. Hebrews 11:6 says, *"And without faith it is impossible to please* [totally satisfy] *Him...."* Your daily use of eyes of faith brings Jesus such satisfaction.

Do you long to please Him? Then reconsider your circumstances and realize that what seems to be a hopeless situation (no prospects on the horizon) is just the flip side of the view through eyes of faith.

Sometimes in an attempt to be a Lady of Faith, one can get sidetracked trying to hurry the "male order delivery" process.

One must admit that it is more likely a woman would find a godly man in a church, at a Christian college, or in a local Bible study. These are obviously good places to find Mr. Right, but the assumption of finding him can result in disillusionment. Hundreds of wonderful single women live and breathe in all the right places, but they remain single.

You may wonder, "How can I be a Lady of Faith when I feel so insecure deep in my heart that God will deliver the goods? What if I have faith in God and end up being 98 and unmarried?" Of course, you would never outright admit that you're not sure you can trust God. That would appear too ungodly! But there's that sneaking fear in the back of your mind: "If I really give up my search and have eyes of faith, God might not give me what I desire, like a husband, a home, and children." God knows when your heart aches for these precious things. But He also knows that these earthly things will not make you secure.

To be sure, your gnawing fears are very common. The enemy knows how common these fears are, and he feeds them by adding a few lies like, "If you give your desire to the Lord, He will send you to outer Burundi where all the men are three feet tall," or, "If you give all your desires to the Lord, you might get married, but you'll definitely not want to take pictures of your fiancé for your friends to see."

FAITH IS NOT IMMUNIZATION AGAINST DOUBTS

"Can I really trust God with all my hopes and dreams? How will I meet Mr. Right if I have eyes of faith? Doesn't God need any help in developing my dreams? What about needing to be in the right place at the right time? How will I meet Mr. Right if I'm not out and about where he might be? I feel the urge to make a mad dash to the next party or to attend the college with the most available men." Such anxious thoughts are based on fears, not faith. "Faith does not eliminate questions. But faith knows where to take them."[3]

"Faith does not eliminate questions. But faith knows where to take them."

You may say you have faith and are just being practical. Are you? What is the opposite of faith? Fear. Who knows that better than the enemy? At the base of his being is the desire to trick you into missing God's best. Satan wants you to believe the lie that cripples faith: God cannot be trusted.

In order to have eyes of faith, you may have to use a spiritual eyewash to remove the debris that the enemy has dropped into your eyes. The Lady of Faith will have times when her secure eyes of faith begin to blink into an anxious twitch of insecure, sensual sight. She can admit her insecurity to her heavenly Fiancé, and He can calm the twitching eyes. Spending some quality time in the Word is the best "eyewash" for eyes of faith.

Romans 10:17 says, *"So faith comes from hearing, and hearing by the word of Christ."* A Lady of Faith may have to spend dateless weekends in male-saturated churches. She can only be content in this trying situation if she has her eyes of faith properly focused on the ultimate relationship—with her heavenly Bridegroom. Datelessness is a common type of debris that irritates the eyes of faith, but the eyewash treatment—quality time with Jesus and reading His Word—is always effective.

DEEP FAITH: A NO-BOZO HEART GUARD

I didn't have a Christian mother or father. I lived in a deeply disturbed home. But my time in God's Word fortified my heart and developed a No-Bozo Heart Guard in the context of family and friends who were not pursuing Jesus.

The challenges you are facing as a single requires strong faith, and faith is inextricably linked to one's daily "face time" with God.

Here's a quote my beloved college mentor shared with me almost forty years ago. It is still true today:

There is no success, no happiness, and no fulfillment in life apart from a consistent, daily, growing relationship with Jesus through the Word. –M.E. Cravens[4]

So many singles want to succeed and be happy, but they don't have time in their lives for a "holy habit" of reading God's precious Word. My college professor knew that one can pass school but flunk life without living the principle cited.

DIVINE ENCOUNTER

In contrast to the manipulated "chance rendezvous" of the single woman Orpah, Ruth had a divine encounter that affected not only her marital status, but also biblical history. That first morning in Bethlehem, Ruth "happened to" stop in a field belonging to Boaz. Interestingly enough, the same day, Boaz "just happened" to visit that very same field where Ruth was gathering the leftover grain. Their meeting was neither an accident nor the product of female maneuvering. Instead it was the work of a sovereign God.

God providentially directed Ruth to the field of Boaz. This divine encounter is found in the second chapter of Ruth, verse 3: *"...and she happened to come to the portion of the field belonging to Boaz...."* The verb *happened* in Hebrew means "chanced upon." This leaves no room for manipulation. She had a chance, and her chance transported her into the center of God's will and right to Boaz's field. Boaz was wealthy and available. Ruth did not "have plans" when she chanced upon his field. Ruth's eyes of faith led her to the exact spot where she would meet her Mr. Right, Boaz, whose name means "pillar of strength." (Contrast the meaning of his name to that of her first husband, Mahlon, which means "weak and sickly"! God rewarded Ruth's faith with a husband who was a "pillar of strength.")

If Jesus wants you married, He will orchestrate the encounter. You have nothing to fear except getting in His way and trying to "write the script" rather than following His. Jesus does have your best interest at heart. He desires to bless you by giving you the best. Sometimes what you perceive as the best is nothing more than a generic version. Consider His wisdom and love in comparison to your own wisdom and self-love. In whom are you going to trust—all Wisdom and Everlasting Love or little ol' finite you? Ever since the Garden of Eden, women have often felt they could and should know as much as God. Much pain in our world has resulted from dependence on our wisdom rather than on our Father's.

MEETING ACROSS CONTINENTS

A beautiful airline flight attendant left her secular job and went to Germany as a missionary. Her eyes of faith sometimes twitched as the reality of no prospects, especially English-speaking ones, continued to loom before her while she diligently served the Lord. At a Bible conference, she met a single guy who served the Lord on the other side of the world. He was an unlikely candidate according to sensual sight and basic logic, but a long-distance courtship began, and they eventually married. Today they serve the Lord together in the Philippines.

GOD HAS NOT LOST YOUR ADDRESS

Your circumstances and geographical location do not threaten God's will and purpose. Just as God brought Eve to Adam, Rebekah to Isaac, Ruth to Boaz, and someday the Bride of Christ to Himself, He will one day bring Mr. Right to you if you are to be married. This is true regardless of your unique situation. Your location or your occupation may not make you very accessible to available godly men, but these roadblocks do not handicap God. Time and time again, we have had the privilege of watching God bring a wonderful, godly guy into the life of a Lady of Faith. He seems to suddenly appear out of nowhere.

One young lady faithfully attended her church for years. Often she needed to be reminded that "He's just not here yet." God brought her Boaz from across the country to where she was in Florida. This single woman had developed better than 20/20 vision in relation to her eyes of faith. Many tears of faith had washed away the debris that often caused her to doubt if she would ever get married. She used those times of doubting to grow in faith as she turned to God who orchestrated the future blessing for her.

God brought His best for one woman all the way from Escondido, California, to Kenya, Africa, where she was serving her Lord. She was not anxious about the absence of available men. After a broken engagement and a couple of years of less-than-satisfying dating, Vivian had volunteered to go to Kenya, Africa, to teach missionary children. Just before she left for Kenya, she attended a Bible study where she met a precious Christian guy named David. Had she not been leaving for Africa that week, they might have had time to become better acquainted. Frustrated by the reality of meeting such a fine Christian guy just before leaving to go halfway around the world, Vivian followed the Lord to Africa with eyes of faith. Little did she know the script God had written. Halfway through her first term on the field, a construction team arrived from the United States to do some work for the academy where she taught. Guess who was part of the team? You got it: David. He and Vivian not only got acquainted, but they also married right there in Kenya. Just as Jesus brought David to Vivian, Jesus can bring your life-mate to you, no matter where you live.

THE ULTIMATE LADY OF FAITH

The ultimate demonstration of Ladies of Faith are the single women who have lived the ten principles in this book—and who themselves continue in a state of singleness. They have not numbed their longing to be married; instead, they have embraced their Lord so tightly that they face their prolonged singleness with peace, not bitterness. They are thriving, not just surviving singleness.

One woman named DeDe has allowed her heavenly Bridegroom to sustain her through more than forty years as a single. She has never stopped desiring a husband and children, but they are not the focus of her life. Her focus is on the "daily bundle" God gives her. Her daily bundles are specific assignments to love and encourage the people in her world. Instead of having her own baby wrapped in a bundle, the Lord gives her someone else's child to love and encourage (she is the vice principal of a Christian school). Rather than having a husband to wrap her arms around, she has teachers to give hugs and thoughtful notes to during their demanding and draining days. This Lady of Faith has not only pleased her heavenly Bridegroom, but also been a blessing to the Bride of Christ.

(Update: DeDe is now DeDe Kendall—she married my brother-in-law! My husband, Ken, led DeDe to Jesus as a teenager and then, twenty-six years later, married her to his own brother, Gary. My best friend, who has taught *Lady in Waiting* to thousands, is now my sister-in-law!)

Have you hesitated about taking a new job or even going to a foreign mission field because you might miss Mr. Right? Have you passed up opportunities to serve in another Sunday school department because you might miss meeting the man of your dreams? If you are trying to orchestrate the "divine encounter," you might be setting yourself up for a disappointing crash.

Wherever you are, whatever your circumstances may be, whether divorced, widowed, or single and getting older every day, be assured that God has not lost your address or your file. He knows exactly where you are and what you need. Remember, God has already taken care of your greatest need—your salvation—and as Romans 8:32 reminds us, *"He who did not spare His own Son, but delivered Him up for us all, how will He not also with Him freely give us all things?"*

You make the most important decision in life, giving your life to Jesus Christ, "by faith." The second most important decision concerns your life-mate. This decision also demands the element of faith. Waiting for one's life-mate and then saying "I do" to him demands secure faith, like Ruth's faith in the God of Israel.

RUTH AND A KIDNAPPED GIRL— TWO HEARTS OF FAITH

As you know, the Book of Ruth is named after its leading lady. This leading lady had a heart of faith that is profoundly displayed in the first chapter of the book. In it, Ruth leaves not only her family and friends but also her hometown to travel to a nation, people, country, and town of strangers who, quite frankly, were not fans of her nationality. Ruth, a Moabite, was leaving hometown security for a new home with Naomi that would require daily faith. Her faith ultimately led her to say *no* to the gods of her childhood and *yes* to the one true God.

> *But Ruth said, "Do not urge me to leave you or turn back from following you; for where you go, I will go, and where you lodge, I will lodge. Your people shall be my people, and your God, my God"* (Ruth 1:16).

The faith Ruth displayed would lead her to the field where she would meet her Mr. Right and quickly enter her "happily ever after."

Now I will introduce you to another displaced girl whose faith is also an inspiration. Both of these females had hearts of faith that sustained each of them in a new place, a new country, among new people.

Here is the second girl's story. She is one of my heroes. In the fifth chapter of Second Kings, we read about the healing of the leper, Naaman. Most readers focus on the famous commander's healing. Naaman had leprosy and was healed by the prophet after dipping in the Jordan seven times.

> *So he went down and dipped himself seven times in the Jordan, according to the word of the man of God; and his flesh was restored like the flesh of a little child and he was clean* (2 Kings 5:14).

But this miracle was preceded by another miracle often missed by the untrained eye! Let's see if you can spot it:

Now Naaman, captain of the army of the king of Aram, was a great man with his master, and highly respected, because by him the Lord had given victory to Aram. The man was also a valiant warrior, but he was a leper. Now the Arameans had gone out in bands and had taken captive a little girl from the land of Israel; and she waited on Naaman's wife. She said to her mistress, "I wish that my master were with the prophet who is in Samaria! Then he would cure him of his leprosy." Naaman went in and told his master, saying, "Thus and thus spoke the girl who is from the land of Israel" (2 Kings 5:1-4).

Did you catch the miracle? Did you see the miracle of a young Israelite girl who was kidnapped, taken to a foreign land, and made to be a servant? This girl was not bitter. Did she not miss her family and her hometown? Was she not a victim of heartless kidnapping? *Yes, yes, yes!* But according to what the Scripture tells us about her, this young girl did not let bitterness define her. She did not hold on to unforgiveness like a treasured heirloom.

Rather, she professed confidence in the healing God of Israel, and she boldly declared this to her mistress! Somehow this girl had been raised with such a confidence in Jehovah-Rapha (The Lord Who Heals), that even in cruel captivity, she could not hide her faith in God. Talk about a faith-filled single girl! She did not let her circumstances keep her from being profoundly used by God. Are you moaning about your singleness and allowing that mindset to keep you from being a vehicle for a miracle?

This girl had been raised with such a confidence in Jehovah-Rapha (The Lord Who Heals), that even in cruel captivity, she could not hide her faith in God. Talk about a faith-filled single girl!

Before you read any further, if you have been full of doubts and anxiety in reference to your future mate, take a few moments to confess your doubts to God and ask His Spirit to develop in your life this quality of faith. Your faith during the "waiting period" pleases God.

Don't fear or resent the waiting periods in your life. These are the very gardens where the seeds of faith blossom. Whenever circumstances stimulate you to deepen your faith, don't resist them; instead, embrace them willingly. Elisabeth Elliot says in *Passion and Purity* (a must-read for those who are having an anxiety attack during their extended waiting periods):

> I do know that waiting on God requires the willingness to bear uncertainty, to carry within oneself the unanswered question, lifting the heart to God about it whenever it intrudes upon one's thoughts.[5]

Whenever the "unanswered question" captures your mind, or you are overtaken by the restlessness of singleness, take a moment to commit that care where it belongs. As First Peter 5:7 says, *"casting all your anxiety on Him, because He cares for you."* This intruding anxiety about your lack of a life-mate is not reality, but rather a weakness that the Greater Reality is capable of handling. Just go to Jesus as soon as the intruder arrives. Such a practice will only enhance your life as a Lady of Faith.

Many single women have not recognized that the trying, frustrating waiting period is the perfect classroom for the Lady of Faith. Don't skip class! Embrace those dateless nights and, by faith, rest in His faithfulness. The faith you develop as a single will be the best dowry you will bring into your marriage.

Faith…
a fruit whose blossoming aroma
inspires one to victory,
and sustains one after loss. —JMK

Becoming a Lady of Faith

- Go through selected Psalms and circle the words *trust* and *rely upon* in red. Notice David's trust in God. This exercise will strengthen your eyes of faith. What are two other ways to strengthen your faith?

- Can you see the parallel between a strong devotional life and the Lady of Faith? (Read Romans 10:17.)

- Can you see a parallel between your own journey of faith and your daily quiet time with God?

- Read through Hebrews 11 and underline all the verbs. Then go back through and confess, "By faith I can _____," filling in the blank with the verbs from each verse.

- Is there anything you can think of that you can't do by faith?

- Can you trust God to sovereignly bring you together with a Boaz?

- What causes you to struggle in your walk of faith?

- Explain how you tend to manipulate your rendezvous with men and/or how you can allow God to be your heavenly dating service.

- Can you see how an extended period of singleness serves as a great opportunity to develop into a Lady of Faith? Explain.

ENDNOTES

1. http://www.oprah.com/relationships/Top-20-Cities-to-Find -Single-Men; accessed 9/24/13.

2. *USA Today*, April 10, 1990, 4.

3. Elisabeth Elliot, *A Chance to Die* (Old Tappan, NJ: Fleming H. Revell Company, 1987), 117.

4. One of my mentors, M.E. Cravens, a statement made in 1975. Also, see my book, *The Mentoring Mom* (Birmingham, AL: New Hope Publishers, 2006), 68.

5. Elisabeth Elliot, *Passion and Purity* (Old Tappan, NJ: Fleming H. Revell Company, 1984), 59–60.

Chapter 4

LADY OF VIRTUE

What we attract reveals our heart. —JMK

One of life's most costly and beautiful objects is born out of pain and irritation—the pearl. A tiny piece of sand slips into an oyster's shell and begins to rub against the soft tissue, causing irritation. In response to the irritation, the oyster produces a hard substance. This substance eventually develops into one of the world's most beautiful jewels—a lovely luminous pearl. In fact, the greater the irritation, the more valuable the pearl!

Like the oyster, Ruth experienced many irritations or trials in her young life. She grieved the deaths of her father-in-law and husband. She bravely faced the turmoil of change in the direction of her life as well as a move to a foreign land with a bitter mother-in-law. When she arrived in that strange land, the trials did not end. She was immediately thrown into a new working situation among total strangers with new customs. Through all this stress, her new faith began to wrap itself around the painful situations. The by-product was a pearl from the washbasin of Moab.

Through all this stress, her new faith began to wrap itself around the painful situations. The by-product was a pearl from the washbasin of Moab.

Many single women view themselves as ugly oyster shells lying on the beaches of life, beset with the trials and problems that come with not being married. To make matters worse, they compare their crusty exterior to all the beautiful seashells around them and wonder how any man could ever give his attention to them.

If you are one of these women, be encouraged. Don't view the trials of singleness as irritating grains of sand to be discarded as quickly as possible. Realize that God has them there to create something beautiful in you. James 1:2-4 says:

> *Consider it all joy, my brethren, when you encounter various trials, knowing that the testing of your faith produces endurance. And let endurance have its perfect result, that you may be perfect and complete, lacking in nothing.*

God is using the sands of singleness to make you perfect and complete. He's developing pearls of character in your life. He knows that whatever you use to "catch" a guy, you must also use to keep him. If you attract a guy with only your looks, then you are headed for trouble, since looks don't last. As time goes on, we all end up looking like oysters. Therefore, what you look like on the inside is far more important than what you look like on the outside.

SIMPLY IRRESISTIBLE

Consider again our Lady in Waiting. What enabled Ruth to catch Boaz's attention? Was it her gorgeous hair or beautiful eyes? No! The answer is found in Boaz's response to her question in Ruth chapter 2.

> *Then she fell on her face, bowing to the ground and said to him, "Why have I found favor in your sight that you should take notice of me, since I am a foreigner?" Boaz replied to her, "All that you have done for your mother-in-law after the death of your husband has been fully reported to me, and how you left your father and mother and the land of your birth, and came to a people that you did not previously know"* (Ruth 2:10-11).

Boaz was attracted to the virtue and character displayed in Ruth's life. A woman of virtue is irresistible to a godly man.

At a singles conference, one pastor's wife spoke of her life as a child. She grew up with a harsh alcoholic father. He left the family without a penny when she was a young teen. Her outward appearance was very plain, and she could not afford fancy clothing, makeup, or expensive hairstyles. She had very little time to socialize because she had to work to support her family. Instead of feeling bitterness over the rejection she had experienced or frustration over her lack of material possessions and free time, she trusted God to take care of her. She developed a strong prayer life and asked God to make her beautiful. She worked hard and grew strong in faith, believing that God would provide all she needed.

Her testimony was stirring, but the real climax came the next day as her husband spoke. He said, "My wife's character is what caught my attention. Her inner beauty was irresistible. Now, thirty years of marriage and half a dozen children later, I am more attracted to and in love with her than when I first met her." This lady gained her knight's attention with lasting godly character. Today their marriage and ministry remain strong and blessed because of the qualities she allowed God to develop in her while she was single.

An ugly oyster shell is an unlikely place to find a lovely gem, but Isaiah 55:8 says, *"For My thoughts are not your thoughts, nor are your ways My ways...."* You may see an ugly shell, but God sees the beauty He is creating in you. Are the sands of singleness causing you bitterness right now, or are you allowing these trials to change you into a pearl? The Lord wants you to be a Lady of Virtue—a costly, beautiful pearl for all to admire.

YOU CAN'T ATTRACT A BOAZ UNTIL YOU ARE A RUTH

One day I was listening to Dr. Laura Schlessinger counsel a concerned father on the radio about the Bozo his daughter was dating. He said the guy wasn't exactly a knight in shining armor. Then Dr. Laura said something painful but profound: "Sir, your daughter is seeking the level she is at." I have said the same thing to many parents who are upset about the people their children are dating. I always say, "We attract what we are."

Your latest steady date is a reflection of your own heart. If you find only Bozos attracted to you, it's time to investigate. What keeps you from catching the eye of a Boaz? You can't attract what you aren't yourself.[1]

IS VIRTUE EXTINCT IN THE 21ST CENTURY?

In the 21st century, the word *virtue* is not a regular guest in the mainstream vocabulary or colloquial speech. Virtue is probably perceived as a word for the Puritan period of American history and totally out of date today. One of the primary definitions of the word *virtue* is "moral excellence." I know our society is all about "excellence," but it has tried to divorce itself from the *moral* aspect of any excellence.

The leading man in the Book of Ruth was drawn to the leading lady because of the obvious virtue displayed in her life through her choices. In modern times like ours, virtue is not what most guys are concerned about; they are often too busy looking at the exterior and are not even concerned about the interior. And certainly a Bozo is more concerned about a girl's "headlights" and "taillights" than the moral excellence of her heart.

I first heard that terminology from a young, rookie baseball player who played for the Atlanta Braves. He told his chaplain, "I *want* to look on women in purity, but they keep flashing their headlights and taillights—making it almost impossible to look at a woman and not lust!" During the past few years, I've gotten the impression that my ideals are becoming so outdated that people may not want to listen to my ranting and raving about this flashing of headlights and taillights. But this young ball player, like other Boaz guys, *wants* to live honorably! Yet, honestly, he needs help from us women and—take note—even young girls.

I have made a covenant with my eyes not to look lustfully at a girl (Job 31:1 NIV).

No wonder God described Job as a blameless man. A man who can resist lusting after local "eye candy" is indeed a noble creature. Job was a Boaz ahead of his time.

THE BODY-BEAUTIFUL TRAP

The world has convinced many Christians that the only way to get a man's attention is through a gorgeous body. Hollywood has sold the lie that a woman will never marry the man of her dreams if she is not pretty enough or slim enough or tall enough or if she does not have high enough cheek bones! Most dateless women think their condition is the result of the reflection in the mirror. Consequently, women spend millions of dollars every year believing the myth that physical beauty is mandatory for marriage.

Proverbs describes how a woman with no character got a man's attention. Some of the descriptives used for her include the following: smooth tongue, captivating eyes, persuasive and seductive speech, a mouth smoother than oil, and flattering speech (see Prov. 5:3; 6:24-25; 7:21). The techniques used today by the modern woman are as old as the first woman who ever snared a man's soul. The whole emphasis is on the superficial, external aspects of a woman— aspects that fade with every passing day. Many women's magazines glorify this woman's techniques rather than expose her bitter end. Marriage based simply on outward beauty can lead to immorality and, ultimately, divorce when an even more attractive body comes along.

A BLOGGER WHO CONFRONTS SUPERFICIAL EYE CANDY

A while ago I saw a post on Facebook written by a young woman venting about ideals that are sorely not understood by most teenagers.

Her ranting reminded me of all the principles that I am trying to teach teens, college students, and singles. It was so much fun to look up this young woman, see her *youth*, and realize that we are on the same page. Three decades separate us, yet we are shouting the same truths from the mountaintops! Here is a glimpse of what this young woman posted on her blog:

> *...If you choose to wear shirts that show off your breasts, you will attract boys*. To be more specific, you will attract the kind of boys that like to

look down girls' shirts. If you want to date a guy who likes to look at other girls' breasts and chase skirts, then great job; keep it up. *If you don't* want to date a guy who ogles at the breasts of other women, then maybe you should stop offering your own breasts up for the ogling. All attention is not equal. You think you want attention, but you don't. You want respect. All attention is not equal....

Don't play coy or stupid or helpless to get attention. Don't pretend something is too heavy so that a boy will carry it for you. Don't play dumb to stroke someone's ego. Don't bat your eyelashes in exchange for attention and expect to be taken seriously, ever. You can't have it both ways. Either you show the world that you have a brain and passions and skills, or you don't. There are no damsels in distress managing corporations, running countries, or managing households. The minute you start batting eyelashes, eyelashes is all you've got....

You are beautiful. You are enough. The world we live in is twisted and broken, and for your entire life you will be subjected to all kinds of lies that tell you that you are not enough. You are not thin enough. You are not tan enough. You are not smooth, soft, shiny, firm, tight, fit, silky, blonde, hairless enough. Your teeth are not white enough. Your legs are not long enough. Your clothes are not stylish enough. You are not educated enough. You don't have enough experience. You are not creative enough.

There is a beauty industry, a fashion industry, a television industry, (and most unfortunately) a pornography industry: and all of these have unique ways of communicating to bright young women: you are not beautiful, sexy, smart or valuable enough....

You are beautiful. You are valuable. You are enough.[2]

The Word of God very clearly warns women not to fall into the body-beautiful trap: *"Your beauty should not come from outward adornment, such as braided hair and the wearing of gold jewelry and fine clothes"* (1 Pet. 3:3 NIV). Although braided hair and gold jewelry are not wrong in and of themselves, real beauty is not found on the outside. This verse does not advocate homeliness as proof of godliness. Some women are under the misguided perception that to be holy, one must look homely. This is not true. Women should seek to look their best. This verse simply challenges you to not devote all your energies toward painting the outside, thus neglecting the enduring qualities that need developing on the inside.

Modesty is presenting yourself so that the attention of other people is drawn to your face not your body. –Pastor Jimmy Scroggins

---

The key to beauty is found in First Peter 3:4 (NIV): *"Instead, it should be that of your inner self, the unfading beauty of a gentle and quiet spirit, which is of great worth in God's sight."* This kind of beauty can only get better the older it gets. As Jackie once said, "If a man chose me for external beauty, his destiny would be hugging a prune. But, if a man chooses me for my internal beauty, his destiny will be unfading beauty even in the twilight years of marriage, because of Jesus."

When you look at the virtuous woman of Proverbs 31:10-31, you will see God's picture of a beautiful woman. There are twenty verses describing her. Only one verse mentions her outward appearance. If you were to spend 1/20th of your time on outward physical beauty and the other 19/20ths on developing the other qualities God describes as beautiful, such as wisdom, kindness, and godliness, you would become the excellent woman Proverbs 31:10 says a man should try to find.

Remember what King Solomon said in Proverbs 31:30 (NIV) about the external emphasis of charm and glitz? *"Charm is deceptive, and beauty is fleeting; but a woman who fears the Lord is to be praised."* There are many women who fear pimples, wrinkles, flabby thighs, and crow's feet, but very few women who really fear the Lord. With which are you attractive to men: the snares of Proverbs 5, 6, and 7, or the beauty of First Peter 3:4?

FIT FOR A KING

When you picture the perfect man for you, what is your prince like? Do you see a man devoted to God? A man of character—teachable, loyal, faithful, gentle, and kind? What kind of woman do you think this godly man desires to marry—a shallow woman or a woman full of charm who knows how to dress and capture other men's attention? Is this the one he imagines he will one day want to spend the rest of his life with—the mother of his heirs? No way!

To marry a prince, you must first become a princess. To marry into royalty, you must be appropriately prepared. Even Kate Middleton had to go through a period of "waiting and preparing" before marrying Prince William. She had to learn how to properly act, dress, and speak so she would honor the royal family. Is it any wonder that a heavenly princess must prepare inwardly for the calling to which she will give her life? As you set your attention on developing godly character, Christ will change you into the beautiful princess He created you to be.

Ruth is not the only biblical example of a Lady in Waiting who developed into God's virtuous pearl. Consider the story of the lovely Rebekah in Genesis.

The girl was very beautiful, a virgin, and no man had had relations with her; and she went down to the spring and filled her jar and came up. Then the servant ran to meet her, and said, "Please let me drink a little water from your jar." And she said, "Drink, my lord"; and she quickly lowered her jar to her hand, and gave him a drink. Now when she had finished giving him a drink, she said, "I will draw also for your camels until they have finished drinking." So she quickly emptied her jar into the trough, and ran back to the well to draw, and she drew for all his camels. Meanwhile, the man was gazing at her in silence, to know whether the Lord had made his journey successful or not. When the camels had finished drinking, the man took a gold ring weighing a half-shekel and two bracelets for her wrists weighing ten shekels in gold, and said, "Whose daughter are you? Please tell me, is there room for us to lodge in your father's house?" She said to him, "I am the daughter of Bethuel, the son of Milcah, whom she bore to Nahor." Again she said to him, "We have plenty of both straw and feed, and room to lodge in" (Genesis 24:16-25).

The "pickins were slim" in Rebekah's shepherding community. Worse than that, she worked full time for her father tending sheep! As you read her story though, there is good indication that Rebekah was doing more than "just waiting." Look at the endearing qualities she developed for her unknown knight (Isaac).

Genesis 24:15-16 shows that Rebekah was a hard worker with a *"jar on her shoulder"* serving her dad's sheep. She also was *"a virgin, and no man had had relations with her."* She had not settled for second best in her wait. She had been under her father's authority and in her father's home serving his interests. Her respect for others showed in her kindness to a stranger in verse 18: *"'Drink, my lord'; and she quickly lowered her jar to her hand, and gave him a drink."* This was no slow, lazy woman, but one with the character quality of genuine care for someone in need. She had character like "Ruby" in Proverbs 31:20: *"She extends her hand to the poor, and she stretches out her hands to the needy."*

REBEKAH'S SERVANT HEART—IRRESISTIBLE

Rebekah did not stop after one act of kindness either! *"...I will draw also for your camels until they have finished drinking"* (Gen. 24:19). Rebekah had initiative and served without even being asked. She was not being manipulative with her service either. This was not a plan to get a man. She was not initiating service and working with such gusto for the reward of a young man's attention. She was treating a smelly old traveler and his dusty, cantankerous camels special because that was her character! She was attentive to the needs of those around her and sought to meet them. She didn't offer them a sip of water, just doing a halfway job—she waited until they were finished drinking.

Look at her diligence in verse 20: *"So she quickly emptied her jar into the trough, and ran back to the well to draw, and she drew for all his camels."* She was a gracious, giving woman, as Genesis 24:25 says: *"Again she said to him, 'We have plenty of both straw and feed, and room to lodge in.'"*

The servant had found a wife for his master's son completely on her virtuous character. She wasn't even in Isaac's neighborhood trying to meet him. She was busy with her father's sheep, but God brought them together.

When the servant made his intentions known and wanted her to leave with him in Genesis 24:54-57, Rebekah knew she had been in the Lord's school of preparation, and she was ready. Her answer was, *"I will go"* (Gen. 24:58). Are you becoming a virtuous woman who a man may need as a helpmate? Are you using these days to develop godliness in order that, if asked, you will be ready? Whether you marry or not, every woman should seek the virtues of Christlikeness.

Rebekah's story closes with the perfect ending to a love story: *"Isaac...lifted up his eyes.... Rebekah lifted up her eyes, and when she saw Isaac she dismounted.... Then Isaac brought her into his mother Sarah's tent...and she became his wife, and he loved her..."* (Gen. 24:63-64,67). God rewarded this virtuous woman's wait with her dream come true. The wait was worth it. Isaac loved the woman who waited for him.

**God desires that every man and woman develop
their inner lives so that through the passing years and
fading of outward beauty, their love still deepens and grows.**

If Rebekah had not developed godly character, would Isaac have been so attracted to her? Perhaps for a time, but within marriage, the real man and woman comes out. That can be a wonderful or a horrible experience. God desires that every man and woman develop their inner lives so that through the passing years and fading of outward beauty, their love still deepens and grows. Are you developing into a woman who will be able to live "happily ever after"?

TO TELL THE TRUTH

Beware What You Wear

I find it ironic that a woman will dress provocatively for a date but be insulted if the man wants to fondle what she has boldly displayed.

A dear friend teaches on abstinence. She likens this behavior to placing a box of Krispy Kreme donuts on her chest. Then she talks about trying to hold a conversation with a starving man—without his wanting to paw the donut box. For a woman to display herself and expect a healthy man to not want to touch what is on display is so foolish.

My son, Ben, agrees: "Since I am a guy, I am really visual, so when a girl dresses like a hooker, it does not matter what comes out of her mouth…she has already told me all I want to know about her. The way girls dress—the more skin the guy sees—the less he is thinking about her as a person and the more she becomes an object. Guys have one-track minds. How [women] dress determines what track we get on. We're either on the get-to-know-you-as-a-person track or on the get-to-know-your-body track."[3]

So there are two ways to get a man to notice you. The first way, "the body-beautiful trap," is to get his attention by how you look on the outside. This is a snare because looks don't last. They are superficial. The second way is what caused Boaz to notice Ruth and Isaac to be drawn to Rebekah. A Lady of Virtue is noticed because she has gained admiration for her godly character.

Be truthful. Which approach best represents you? Take the following test. Check the items in each column that describe you most often. Score each total of qualities on the two lists to see if you are developing inner or outer beauty most diligently.

Lady of Virtue	Body Beautiful
A person to whom all people are attracted (friendly)	Nice only to those who can help your dating status
Seeking God first	Seeking a relationship first
Interesting—with goals for yourself personally	"Shopping"—known to be looking for a husband
Becoming the lady God wants you to be	Waiting to be found
Realistic	Living in romantic fantasy

(continued)

Lady of Virtue	Body Beautiful
Truly interested in the person you date and his best interests	Looking for your future in the relationship
One who is spiritually challenging	Exciting sensuality
One who gives friendship	One who expects friendship
One who communicates verbally	A wallflower
Committed to trusting God	Clinging to a guy
Prepared for lasting friendships	Playing games
Open to other friendships	Possessive
Secure in the Lord	Insecure without a "dream man"
Building positive qualities in yourself	Wanting him now
Trusting God	Trusting in schemes and plans to catch a man
Patiently waiting	On the hunt
Score yourself:	Score yourself:
(total qualities)	(total qualities)

How did you do? Are you allowing the Holy Spirit to use the sands of singleness to create in you priceless pearls of virtuous character?

Providing lasting pleasure,
potential beyond measure,
the rarest of treasure,
a reputation of virtuous character. —JMK

STRINGING TOGETHER A PEARL NECKLACE

The qualities Ruth and Rebekah displayed do not come from the jewelry store; neither are they activated the day someone places an engagement ring on your finger. Virtue is developed over time as you allow God's Spirit to do a special work in your life.

Pearls of character are "...love, joy, peace, patience, kindness, goodness, faithfulness, gentleness, self-control...."

It is the Holy Spirit, not you, who produces the godly character you seek. These pearls of character are listed in Galatians 5:22-23 as *"...love, joy, peace, patience, kindness, goodness, faithfulness, gentleness, self-control...."* As these qualities develop, your life will become like a beautiful necklace strung with the pearls of godly character.

Galatians 5:19-21, however, describes some "beads" with which many singles choose to adorn their lives instead. They are *"...immorality, impurity, sensuality, idolatry, sorcery, enmities, strife, jealousy, outbursts of anger, disputes, dissensions, factions, envying, drunkenness, carousing, and things like these...."* If you desire to be a Lady of Virtue, these beads cannot belong on your necklace. If you see that you have a bad bead in your strand of pearls, it must be removed and replaced with the character quality that pleases God.

To remove the bad bead, confess the sin that developed this unattractive quality. Be honest with yourself and don't cover over or excuse the sin God shows you. Be specific. For instance, instead of saying, "Forgive me for all my many sins," say, "Lord, I have been envious of __. Forgive me for dwelling on what You have given *her* instead of thanking You for what You have given me." After specifically describing the bead that detracts from your inner beauty, then receive God's forgiveness. His Word says, *"If we confess our sins, He is faithful and righteous to forgive us our sins and to cleanse us from all unrighteousness"* (1 John 1:9). You no longer need to feel condemned or guilty because *"as far as the east is from the west, so far has He removed our transgressions from us"* (Ps. 103:12).

Once you have received God's forgiveness, ask the Lord to cleanse you from whatever caused the sin in the first place. For example, envy often results from comparing yourself to others or from an ungrateful heart. This deeper problem must be changed if envy is to be decisively overcome. If you do not cleanse your heart of these deeper issues, you will find yourself always on your knees asking forgiveness because of a continual struggle with the sin of envy.

One deals with these deeper issues through the power of God's Holy Spirit. He provides the needed power to take care of the deeper issues that produce bad beads. Galatians 5:16 speaks of this when it says, *"...walk by the Spirit, and you will not carry out the desire of the flesh."* How does one walk by the Spirit and tap into this pearl-producing power? Three portions of Scripture make it clear.

The first, Ephesians 4:30, says, *"Do not grieve the Holy Spirit of God."* You grieve or hurt God's Spirit when you choose to think, say, or do something that offends God. To tap into pearl-producing power, you must first decide to live a life that will please your Lord in all respects. From the time you wake in the morning until you go to bed at night, set your heart's desire on exalting Him.

The second verse is found in First Thessalonians 5:19. It says, *"Do not quench the Spirit."* To "quench" gives the word picture of throwing water on a fire. When God's Spirit prompts you to do something, give expression to that impression. Don't douse it with cold water by ignoring His leadership. For example, He may prompt you to perform an act of kindness, or caution you not to say something you are about to say, or lead you to encourage a friend who may be hurting. Whatever it is, seek to obey the Spirit of God in you on a moment-by-moment basis.

Finally, to tap into pearl-producing power, Ephesians 5:18 says, *"...be filled with the Spirit."* To be filled, something must first be empty. To be filled by the Spirit you must be empty of yourself and full of God. You give the Holy Spirit complete and total control of your life. When you became a Christian, you received all of the Holy Spirit. To be a virtuous woman, you must let the Holy Spirit have all of you.

There are many imitations of a true pearl, but with years, the shiny pearl paint cracks and wears off and all that is left is an unattractive bead hanging on a string. God's Spirit, however, produces true inner beauty, as you confess your sin, avoid displeasing God's Spirit, obey even the slightest of His promptings, and give the Holy Spirit full control of your life. Pearls of godly character take time to develop, but how blessed is the woman adorned by them!

You can settle for an imitation necklace of fake pearls by trying to simply cover over ungodly character, or you can allow the Holy Spirit to use the sands of singleness to create the real thing.

You can settle for an imitation necklace of fake pearls by trying to simply cover over ungodly character, or you can allow the Holy Spirit to use the sands of singleness to create the real thing. If you want a cheap imitation, a modeling or charm school will be sufficient for what you seek. But if you want genuine pearls, you must allow the Holy Spirit to perform a special work in your life. Determine to string a lovely pearl "necklace of virtue" as a treasure for your Lord.

IMITATION PEARLS—MISSIONARY DATING

A common self-deception among all women whether young or older is their power to *change* the guy she has a crush on, admires from afar, or has begun to date. Believe me, I've had a thousand conversations with gals trying to explain their reasoning to justify dating nonbelievers. I've even had parents explain what "nice" guys their daughters are dating. I always ask, "Is he a Christian?"

Most parents respond defensively, "I don't know, but he comes from a good family."

When I follow up with the second question: "What do you mean by a good family?" I unfortunately find that, more often than not, *good* means *rich*. Since the first woman ate from the forbidden tree, women have assumed that they are smarter than God and have the power to change those who become the "objects" of their desire.

A sad endnote for this chapter: Two decades ago when this book was published, the following material would not even have been considered for this chapter on virtue! Two decades later, it's sadly something I must address. It is a sensitive topic, but the carnage of broken hearts and lives requires me to address it for the sake of my sisters in Jesus all around the world.

BOZOS AND BOOZE

I could write a separate book of the horror stories I've heard about reckless actions between men and women because of alcohol. I won't spend too much time on this, but suffice it to say, a woman (young or old) who is intoxicated is a perfect match for a Bozo. Be assured: *Bozos are watching for women who like to overdo it.*

Booze makes Bozo men courageous enough to disregard a woman's "no," even if she says it a dozen times.

Booze makes Bozo men courageous enough to disregard a woman's "no," even if she says it a dozen times. Booze has too often been the stimuli for Bozos to consider the unthinkable: to rape a drunken girl or to drug a girl to get sex. What would produce such boldness and perversion? An age of no standards. We are so enlightened, yet simultaneously so blind.

A few years ago I had three precious single gals in my life who were all raped during a drinking party. I know that thousands of girls can go to a party and not be raped, but my friends never even considered the lethal combination of Bozos and booze.

One young man I know wisely says, "When a gal goes to a frat party or even a bar, for her safety she needs to walk in with a bottle of water and consume only that. She should carry her bottle of water around like a security blanket." Girls have more to lose than a credit card when they are around the lethal combination of Bozos and booze. Better yet, women should opt for better places to meet men than bars and frat parties! Where do you think you'll find potential "men worth waiting for"? Go there instead![4]

The Pearl

In every oyster there lies the ability
to produce something rare.
Truth like a grain of sand will produce
the pearl that is hidden there.
Young woman, you are often mocked and scorned,
and told you never should have been born.
You want to run away, to hide your hurt.
Your heart is wounded, bleeding and torn.
God makes not mistakes:
every life is special,
every life is planned.
Seeds can sprout in sand.
Open yourself up to the Spirit of God,
grow in grace and maturity,
be what He wants you to be.
Your beauty, your strength lies deep within you.
Young woman, young girl,
open yourself up to God.
Allow Him to reveal your pearl. —*Sylvia Hannah*

BECOMING A LADY OF VIRTUE

- Is virtue extinct in the 21st century? (Read Jeremiah 6:16 and Amos 8:11-14.)

- Study Rebekah in Genesis 24 and write out all the character qualities you find. Which of these do you need to develop? Pick one of these qualities and describe how you will specifically work on making it real in your life.

- What books have you read dealing with the virtues/disciplines of a godly woman? In contrast, how many magazines have you read that deal with external glamour? What good books can you begin to read that will help develop your own personal godliness?

- Pick out a picture of a woman who, according to magazines, "has everything." What features do you see? What appeal has been used? What is dangerous about comparing yourself with pictures like that?

- Read Proverbs 31. In prayer admit, "Father, You don't choose to zap me into completion. So today I choose to cooperate with the Holy Spirit as You make me a Lady of Virtue. From my Scripture reading, show me one quality from Proverbs 31 that I need to develop." (For example: discipline, thoroughness, graciousness, giving, diligence.) Pray over this quality for a month before moving to something else.

- Examine the "necklace" you are stringing by checking it in the light of Galatians 5:16-24. How many bad beads do you see in your necklace? Confess these sins and ask God's Spirit to control you in these areas. Spend time with a godly friend who will pray for you weekly until the bad beads are replaced by quality pearls.

- Have you defended missionary dating? (Read Second Corinthians 6:14; Joshua 23:12-13.)

- Discuss the quote: "You attract who you are!"

- Discuss the last section on Bozos and Booze.

ENDNOTES

1. Jackie Kendall, *A Man Worth Waiting For* (Nashville, TN: Faith Words, 2008), 15.

2. Kate Elizabeth Conner, "Ten Things I Want to Tell Teenage Girls" Lily Pads, March 25, 2012; http://kateelizabethconner.com/ten-things-i-want-to-tell-teenage-girls/ (accessed 9/27/12). Kate is the mom of two toddlers.

3. Kendall, *A Man Worth Waiting For*, 186.

4. Ibid., 96.

Chapter 5

LADY OF DEVOTION

Rescue me from me, so I might serve Thee.

In the receiving line at her younger sister's wedding, many guests greeted Brenda over and over with teasing remarks. She heard comments such as, "Always a bridesmaid, but never a bride. When is it going to be your turn? The only girl in your dad's home still unmarried!" Though these well-wishers may have been speaking out of fun or even compassion, their speech was not wise. The barrage caused its damage. It is hard enough for a single woman to keep her focus where it should be without friends making insensitive comments.

How much better it would be for the Lady in Waiting if she were encouraged to pursue her undistracted devotion to the Lord Jesus Christ, instead of being made to feel like she does not quite measure up. If Jesus had been one of the guests, He would have surely commended her for productively using her single time to its fullest.

**A Lady in Waiting has the advantage of being able
to develop her love relationship with Christ without
the distractions that a husband or family
inherently bring to one's heart.**

Much too often people view a single woman as though she should be pitied rather than envied. Nothing could be further from the truth. A Lady in Waiting has the advantage of being able to develop her love relationship with Christ without the distractions that a husband or family inherently bring to one's heart.

This has been God's plan from the beginning. He tenderly created woman to love Him and to experience the blessedness of fellowship with Him. In those first days, Eve communed with God in indescribable fellowship and oneness. When God came to walk in the cool of the day, there was no fear, only love. Eve had only positive feelings about God. She loved Him and knew He loved her. She enjoyed Him and devoted herself totally to His pleasure.

God still desires to know and be known by women today. But because sin entered the world, we no longer have a clear picture of the true God. "Satan's first attack upon the human race was his sly effort to destroy Eve's confidence in the kindness of God."[1] Satan lied to Eve about God's character. *"Indeed, has God said...?"* (Gen. 3:1). Satan has continued to lie to Eve's daughters. As a result, fear has often alienated women from the One who loves them as they need to be loved. Deep within a woman's soul remains the longing for the gentle embrace of the God Who Is, not the god that the enemy has craftily devised.

MODELING HOPE OR HOPELESSNESS

Boaz spoke of Ruth's devotion to God when he said, *"May the Lord reward your work, and your wages be full from the Lord, the God of Israel, under whose wings you have come to seek refuge"* (Ruth 2:12). Ruth chose to cling to Naomi's God as her own even though her mother-in-law had drawn a negative, harsh picture of Him:

> She said to them, "Do not call me Naomi [pleasant]; *call me Mara* [bitter], *for the Almighty has dealt very bitterly with me. I went out full, but the Lord has brought me back empty. Why do you call me Naomi, since the Lord has witnessed against me and the Almighty has afflicted me?"* (Ruth 1:20-21)

Would you be devoted to a God like Naomi's? In Naomi's bitterness, she no longer referred to God as "the Lord" as she had in verses 8 and 9, but with a title that can cause one to feel alienated and insignificant—"the Almighty." Though Ruth clung to Naomi as a mother, she did not accept her mother-in-law's view of God for herself. "If we think of Him (God) as cold and exacting, we shall find it impossible to love Him, and our lives will be ridden with servile fear."[2]

FURTHER INSIGHT CONCERNING BITTER NAOMI

During the twenty years since this book was published, I have had more time to look closely at Naomi, aka, "Mara." What God has shown me is that even a bitter woman cannot *hide* her belief in the One True God. Ruth chose to believe and follow the One True God, the Hope of Zion *because* of Naomi's belief in Him. Even when Naomi was whining, the reality of the God in whom she trusted still shone through the cracks in her life.

God has shown me that even on the days when I struggle, the incomparable treasure of Jesus within me will shine through—if only a tiny crack of light.

God has shown me that even on the days when I struggle, the incomparable treasure of Jesus within me will shine through—if only a tiny crack of light. Of course, I would rather Jesus shine through me like a burst of fireworks; but oh, the joy that He shines through me even when I am struggling! His strength is made perfect in our weakness.

Therefore I will boast all the more gladly about my weaknesses, so that Christ's power may rest on me (2 Corinthians 12:9 NIV).

Your past experiences, present circumstances, or your parents' devotion or lack thereof may cause you to have an incorrect view of God. But nothing and no one can give you a clearer picture of the true God than slipping under His wings and discovering for yourself who God really is, the refuge for which you long. He desires for you to come again "into the garden" and walk with Him in complete fellowship. This is the fullness of devotion.

As a single, you have a wonderful opportunity to use your time to maximize your fellowship with God. When you love someone, you give him your heart, the center of your being. God asks for no less. He desires a totally devoted heart. Deuteronomy 6:5 says that you are to love Him with all your heart (deepest devotion), your soul (what you think and what you feel), and your might (your strength and energy).

Many women today are devoted, all right! They have devoted themselves to developing a love relationship, but not with the Lord. They erroneously seek love in sensations and promises. The world's version of love is something they want to "fall into." Meanwhile, "true love" escapes them. True love can only be found in undistracted devotion to Jesus Christ. What is preventing you from living "hopelessly devoted" to Jesus?

DELIVER ME FROM ME

So many singles are simply not thriving in their singleness. They seem to be just barely surviving. What is it that has captured their hearts and stifled their growth in devoted and fruitful singleness?

By definition, to grow in devotion to the Lord is to focus on Him and to seek His heart for His Kingdom. Yet, as we are all too aware, there is another kingdom we like to visit—and camp out in! It is not the beautifully expansive Kingdom of God, but the puny, limited, claustrophobic kingdom of self.

When I became a new Christian, I was introduced to the concept of a life with either *self* in charge or the Holy Spirit in charge. I was constantly asked by my youth leader whether particular behaviors were motivated by self being on the throne of my life, or by the guidance of the Holy Spirit. As the years passed, I heard very little about the impact of self on a person's walk with Jesus, but I was always aware of its obvious manifestation. The Bible clearly defines what this claustrophobic kingdom of self thrives on:

> *The activities of the lower nature are obvious. Here is a list: sexual immorality, impurity of mind, sensuality, worship of false gods, witchcraft, hatred, quarrelling, jealousy, bad temper, rivalry, factions, party-spirit, envy, drunkenness, orgies and things like that* (Galatians 5:19-21 PNT).

These activities may look intimidating, yet they are common behaviors of the me-centric life that is at war with the very life of God within each of His children.

Because we serve the King of kings in a dark and broken world, we are keenly aware of a kingdom that we fight daily. It is a kingdom with walls higher than Jericho and a moat wider than the Pacific Ocean surrounding it. This kingdom is ferociously protected by a warrior that would make Goliath look like a midget.

You might assume that I am writing about the prince of the power of the air (see Eph. 2:2), satan. Although he is the archenemy of our souls, I am thinking of an insidious enemy that is almost too close to notice: the enemy called *self*. This is the part of us the Bible calls the flesh, or the "old man." It is the core of self-centered, self-protective sin that compels us, as Paul writes in Romans, to do what the Christlike self does not want to do.

It is the very work of God in our lives as believers to slay this tyrant and to flourish in our true identity, our true self in Him.

This tyrant of the claustrophobic kingdom of self has harmed our walk with God. However, it is the very work of God in our lives as believers to slay this tyrant and to flourish in our *true* identity, our *true self* in Him. God has given us the spirit of power and love and self-control (see 2 Tim. 1:7); and He has given us the weapons of His Kingdom to aid in our fight.

I have always been aware of the impact of me-centric living, but it was presented in a powerful refresher course when I started reading a book recommended by my son-in-law, Drew. The book, written by Paul Tripp, is entitled, *What Did You Expect?* Here is just a taste:

> In his love, he knows that you are not all that you were created to be. Even though it may be hard to admit, there is still sin inside you, and that sin gets in the way of what you are meant to be and designed to do. And, by the way, that sin is the biggest obstacle of all to a marriage of unity, understanding, and love. God is using the difficulties of the here and now to transform you, *that is, to rescue you from* **you** (emphasis added).³

What a powerful phrase: *"rescue you from you."* All one has to do is watch the news about celebrities and notice the enormous kingdom of self that is applauded and aspired to; yet people are shocked when celebrities make poor choices. The kingdom of self is above the law, and the entitlement that fuels this kingdom began in each person's home. Whether among athletes, rock singers, or movie stars, there are many public displays of the kingdom of self for us to see.

From time to time on long trips in the car, I listen to a radio psychologist on Sirius Satellite Radio. A common phrase that always makes me grin is when the radio personality says to a distraught caller, "Now just a minute, I need you to take yourself out of the center of your universe and take a moment to think about this other person."

This counselor continually confronts the claustrophobic kingdom of self that is dominating the lives of daily callers. So where do these narcissistic people get their training? Such me-centric living is in the heart of every man and woman, boy and girl, enhanced or diminished by those who love them.

> **The kingdom of self is a more toxic environment
> for breeding your struggles than your state
> of datelessness or prolonged singleness!**

It can be challenging to consider this painful reality, but *please* recognize this: the kingdom of self is a more toxic environment for breeding your struggles than your state of datelessness or prolonged singleness!

To love God devotedly, you must know Him intimately. Paul expressed the desire to *"know"* God in Philippians 3:10. In Greek, this word *know* means "a knowledge that perfectly united the subject with the object."[4] Paul was desiring to know God intimately. Second Peter 1:3 says that everything pertaining to life and godliness is yours *"through the true knowledge of Him."* Peter and John in Acts 4:13 were identified as uneducated men, but the people observed their confidence and devotion to the Lord and marveled. In the King James Version of Scripture, the people exclaimed that these men "knew" Him, or that *"they had been with Jesus."* This "knowing" has the same depth as the term in Genesis 4:1 when Scripture speaks of the intimate relations Eve had when she *"knew"* or "had been with" her husband. It is a personal, intimate knowledge.

Do you have a devotion to God that causes people to marvel at how intimately you know Him? Do you know God in a way that causes Him to be an intimate, personal part of your being as you may desire a husband to one day be?

As a woman, you have been created with a desire to be known—not just in a physical or general way, but deeply known and intimately loved. If you are hoping a man will one day fill your heart's desire for intimacy, you will be disappointed. God knows your deep longings for intimate love. Only He, the Lover of your soul, can fill this need completely. Your heavenly Father tenderly created you with needs that only God can fully understand and fulfill. As you come to know who He really is, He will meet your needs for love.

**Your heavenly Father tenderly created you with
needs that only God can fully understand and fulfill.**

Your heavenly Father is incapable of doing evil. He loves you, and forgives and completely forgets confessed sins and grievances. Is this the God you know? You may think you know God, but your responses to God will betray you. If you retract in fear, try to hide things, give excuses when you do something you feel God would not like, then it shows your knowledge of God, like Naomi's, is incorrect. God is not supersensitive, selfish, or temperamental.

Do you ever have a feeling of guilt hanging over your head that you are not doing enough to please God? Do you feel like the scale of expectations is tipping heavily in the negative and you must balance it? Do you feel like you could never do enough to pay for your inability to be perfect? Then your view of God is incorrect. God is not hard to please. He takes delight in His creation and quickly notices every simple effort to please Him (see Ps. 103:11-14).

Do you feel like God requires too much of you? Do you feel like God denies you the things you need most? If you do, then you don't really know God. Psalm 103:8-14 destroys these wrong assumptions about God. Have you lived with lies about God for too long? Get to know Him.

God wants to do you good and not evil. Jeremiah 29:11 says He wants to give you a future and a hope. Has your wrong picture of God been invented by the enemy in order to rob you of a true knowledge and love of God? Do not be deceived as Eve was in the Garden. Get to know the One your heart truly desires to love. To love God, you must know Him intimately, personally, and devotedly. This does not require immediate entrance into a convent; you get to know Him by seeking Him.

SEEKING TRUE LOVE

Seeking God is very similar to developing a friendship. You talk a lot, you listen, you write each other letters, you think about each other, you find out what the other likes and does not like, and you try to do things that please that person. The more you spend time together, the more intimately you know your friend. And the more intimately you know your friend, the greater your love will be. It works the same way with your relationship with God.

Jeremiah 29:12-13 promises that a woman who diligently seeks God with all her heart will find Him. Your heart is the key to devotion to God. To find God, you must seek Him with your whole heart. A halfhearted search is not sufficient. This means you cannot seek God while you do your own thing.

IS GOD DEMANDING TOO MUCH?

Is God demanding too much to require that you seek Him with all your heart? No way! Think of it this way. Mr. Right comes over one day and begins to speak of his devotion to you. He says what you have been waiting to hear: "I love you. I give you my heart completely. For 364 days of every year, I will devote myself to you and you only." But then he adds, "However, *one* day each year I want to date others and see what I have missed. Don't worry; you can have *all* the rest. Will you marry me?"

What would your response be? Would you want this kind of devotion? Would it be selfish of you to deny him his heart just one day a year to give to others? No! Absolutely not. You would want his total love and devotion. You would want his heart all 365 days a year.

Similarly, giving Christ your heart means you are not free to give it away to other things or people that come into your life (in idolatry). You can't give a part to relationships that delight you in this world and still seek God with a *whole* heart. You cannot keep part of your heart for something that may seem better if it comes along. Devotion to the Lord Jesus Christ is giving everything or nothing at all. Your devotion to Christ must be a serious commitment to His Lordship. Christ loves you and is completely committed to you. Wholeheartedly devote yourself to loving and enjoying Him in return, 365 days a year.

If you are to know God intimately, then you must seek Him, not only with a whole heart, but also with a clean heart. When you think of the word *bride*, you probably first imagine a beautiful, clean, pure woman in white. No grime or dirt mars the image of purity. As a Christian you are part of the Bride of Christ. Any grime or dirt of sin will mar your image before Him.

The Lord's fiancé must have a clean heart. You must clean up any blot of sin that may arise between you and your heavenly Sweetheart. Sin causes God to back away from a person. It is disgusting to Him; He will not abide with it. Picture a couple deeply in love. He loves to be near her—so near he can breathe the fresh aroma of her sweet breath! What love! He hates onions, though, especially on his beloved's breath. It really turns him off. What do you think she does before she sees him if she has eaten onions? Well, she wouldn't want the sweetness of their fellowship hindered, so she brushes away what offends him. Not only does she brush, but she also gags on a quart of mouthwash. She doesn't want to offend her love! She wants nothing to come between them.

Sin is far more repulsive to God than even onion breath is to a sweetheart. If you want your devotion to God to be complete, don't merely brush at sin lightly. Get in there and confess it, clean it up, and clear it out. Be rid of it. If you notice you have spiritual halitosis during the day, take care of it immediately. Let Psalm 51:10 be your prayer: *"Create in me a clean heart, O God...."*

Many seek God, but only for His hand. They don't want God as much as they want something from God, such as a man, happiness, or a family. This impure search for God is limited to what you can get. It is more of a self-love than a God-love. This seeking will end in misery, not in the union of love you desire. God cannot be used like your credit card. He knows your motives. To grow in your knowledge of God, you must seek God correctly, which means you must also seek God with a pure heart.

**A woman with a pure heart for God does not
focus on what He gives, but delights in who He is.**

A woman with a pure heart for God does not focus on what He gives, but delights in who He is. She seeks God's *face*, not just His *hand*. Would you want someone to say he loves you just so you would do something for him? To find God, you must seek Him with pure motives. Seek Him for who He is, not just for what He can do for you.

Have you ever tried to develop an intimate relationship with Jana Jabberbox? She's the gal who has lots to say and loves to hear herself say it. You try to say something when she takes a breath—which isn't often—but she keeps right on talking. She never listens. It's a one-way conversation, and you are left out.

Even when someone is very special to you, you do not get too excited with a steady monologue. Listening is an important part of developing a closeness with someone else. If you want to get to know the Lord, you must seek Him not only with a whole, clean, and pure heart, but also with a listening heart.

As you spend time with God during your daily devotional time, learn to listen to Him as you read of His love and thoughts about you in the Bible. Think about what He is saying to you personally. Sit silently and write what impressions come to your listening heart. As you read and study His love letters, the Bible, you begin to see what He really thinks of you and what wonderful plans He has for you. As a result, your devotion grows and grows.

To find God you must seek Him with a whole heart, a pure heart, a clean heart, and a listening heart. Hebrews 11:6 (NIV) says that He *"rewards those who earnestly seek Him."* Does this describe your growing relationship with the Lord?

Singleness does not have to be a curse. Single gals do not have to wear long faces and be pitied until they are finally married. Quite the contrary! Singleness puts you in an advantageous position because, more than likely, you have much more time to seek the Lord now than you will ever have if you marry.

AN ADVANTAGEOUS POSITION

Married women wrestle constantly with having to balance the physical and emotional demands placed on them. All women must learn to balance their priorities, but the single woman's heart is not sent in different directions by the needs of a husband and children.

Before the sun rises, a mother of young children may gingerly creep down the stairs and dig under the pile of unanswered letters and school assignments to find her Bible. "Ahhh! A few moments of undistracted time," she whispers as she opens her Bible. To her chagrin, from the top of the stairs she hears, "Is it morning yet?" She puts her Bible down and whispers for the little early bird to come quietly down. She encourages him to sit with his favorite book, turns to find her Bible, and begins to read (while Junior makes animal noises reading beside her). Suddenly, from upstairs comes the sound of splashing. "Oh no— Mommy! I missed the potty, and it got on me!" Up the stairs she races to free the soggy victim, mop the floor, wake the school-age child, and get breakfast for everyone.

Her husband needs a button on his shirt, help finding his keys, and dinner an hour early. The kids need an arbitrator, a chauffeur, a nurse—and their P.E. clothes to be washed immediately. She sorts her way through piles of unwashed clothes cluttering the bedroom, trips over toys in the hall, and shovels aside newspapers and coloring books to collapse on the couch for a minute, only to be roused by screams from the children as the day's first civil war breaks out.

Phone calls and drop-in visits continue to interrupt her day at every turn. It is midnight before she finally gets to the dirty dishes...and where is her undistracted time for devotion? If she was a wise Lady in Waiting and used her singleness to develop her devotional life, she has resources that allow her to commune with God during the wildest of days. A wife/mother may find her day beginning early and ending late, often before she has had any uninterrupted time to seek her heart's True Love.

A single woman can choose to cherish the single time instead of feeling unhappy with it. The Word of God illustrates the advantageous position of the single woman in relation to the affairs of life:

> *An unmarried woman or virgin is concerned about the Lord's affairs: Her aim is to be devoted to the Lord in both body and spirit. But a married woman is concerned about the affairs of this world—how she can please her husband* (1 Corinthians 7:34 NIV).

God says the unmarried woman has the advantage when it comes to her devotion to the Lord. An unmarried woman can give the Lord what a married woman rarely can—undistracted devotion.

An unmarried woman can give the Lord what a married woman rarely can—undistracted devotion.

The time to develop a consistent devotional life cannot wait until you marry. Many single women waste valuable years as they wait "for life to begin"—after marriage. Ask any wife, even without children, and she will tell you her own juggling routine. A married woman struggles to have time alone with herself, much less time alone with God.

GLORY ROBBER VERSUS THE LADY OF DEVOTION

We had a guest last summer who was such a blessing that her visit seemed much too short. During hours of sharing heart to heart, I told her about a new message I was developing entitled "Glory Robbers." I explained that, although we were created to bring God glory, we constantly rob Him of the glory He is due. Too many Christians have made their lives so me-centric that they daily rob His glory.

Everyone who is called by My name, whom I created for My glory... (Isaiah 43:7 NIV).

After our wonderful guest left, she pondered the "Glory Robber" theme and she sent the following message:

Being a glory robber is like being a bridesmaid who is more worried about making herself look good than making sure the bride and groom look good and have all they need. I was a bridesmaid back in May; I watched all of the other bridesmaids getting ready and worrying about how *they* looked and such. I just kept thinking, "No one is even going to be looking at us; we are delusional if at any point in this wedding we think it is about *us* as bridesmaids." And then it ticked me right off when the bridesmaids were really only conveniently around when the photographers or videographers were around, but they were nowhere to be seen when it was time to take down the reception hall or unload trucks back at home. Glory robbers often serve the Bride of Christ and the Groom when it is convenient for them or publicity is involved.

Let's not be like the delusional, me-centric bridesmaids in the story. May we resist the temptation to be "ovation-aholics" and instead strive to be true servants of the King. Such servants are comfortable with esteeming others as more important than themselves (see Phil. 2:3).

A Lady of Devotion knows how to bring glory to God and not rob Him of such glory!

Becoming a Lady in Waiting, devoted to loving, knowing, and seeking God, will not come cheaply. You are the one who determines the depth of your relationship with God. He does not have favorites. You must choose to pursue the Lover of your soul—your heavenly Fiancé.

A single woman, one who chose to take advantage of her singleness, wrote the following poem:

The Single Gift

> *How blessed you are, you single one,*
> *Don't talk of care and woes.*
> *You've got too much to be thankful for,*
> *Oh what, you'd like to know.*
> *It's no mistake, no misdirection*
> *Of God's perfect plan*
> *That you've not found your special lady*
> *Or you, that certain man.*

God loves you so and has much more
To give than you've ever received.
That He's giving His best to you right now,
You really must believe.
His best is Himself, do you have it in full,
Or only a bit on the side?
No man can meet your needs like God,
Nor can a lovely bride.
If your life's not complete, you know that Jesus is
And your life He will fill
If you'll only put Him first each day
And live to do His will.
He's gifted you for undistracted
Devotion to the Lord.
There should be nothing that can interfere
With Him and prayer and the Word.
Unless you let down the guard of your heart
And let others take His place,
Then you'll lack joy and peace and hope
And not experience His grace.
So give your heart right back to God,
Let Him keep it safe for you.
And when it's better than His best,
He'll make your one into two. —Donna L. Mihura

God has given you a precious, privileged time. Don't waste a day of it! You will never have it again. These days can be treasure-finding days in your kingly Father's chambers. As you linger at the window ledge searching for a glimmer of your knight's shining armor, don't miss the jewels your Father has for you to adorn yourself. Will you grow cold and bitter at the window sill, or will you hold your royal head high, glowing in your Father's love and attention?

The choice remains with you, dear princess. Your Father will not force you to turn from the window, but He longs to fellowship with you. Come into His chambers, delight in His Presence. May you be found in Him—a Lady of Devotion.

BECOMING A LADY OF DEVOTION

- Read Deuteronomy 30:11-20. What are the benefits of devotion to Christ? What are the results of living a life not devoted to Christ?

- What warnings does God give about your heart in Deuteronomy 11:16 and Deuteronomy 30:17? What gods seek to distract your heart?

- How did David seek God in Psalm 63? What was his reward?

- How is your heavenly courtship progressing? How can you make it better?

- Have you come to a place where your relationship with Jesus is beyond comparison with any earthly love?

- Does your daily devotional relationship with Jesus satisfy you from the top of your head to the bottom of your toes?

- Are you following hard after Jesus, or every eligible guy?

- Read Song of Solomon 6:1. Does your love relationship with Jesus cause your friends to seek after Him as the Shulammite woman's praises did her friends? Why or why not? What can you do differently?

- If you have never spent a consistent devotional time with God before now, begin by reading a psalm a day. After reading the psalm, write answers to these three questions in a notebook:

1. What does this passage say about me?

2. What does this passage say about the Lord?

3. How can it apply to me?

    •   Discuss the impact of the kingdom of self.

    •   Are you guilty of being a Glory Robber?

ENDNOTES

1. A.W. Tozer, *The Root of the Righteous* (Camp Hill, PA: Christian Publications, 1986), 5.

2. Ibid.

3. Paul Tripp, *What Did You Expect?* (Wheaton, IL: Crossway, 2010), 22.

4. W.E. Vine, *Vine's Expository Dictionary of New Testament Words* (Westwood, NJ: Barbour, 1985), 639.

Chapter 6

LADY OF PURITY

No one was surprised when Tim and Susan began dating. They seemed just right for each other. They could talk about anything and had the same ideals for a strong Christian dating relationship. After a year of steady dating, Susan realized how deeply she loved Tim. She wanted to be his wife. She began to show her affection for him in different ways. They began to kiss and touch a little. She felt this was all right. She rationalized that she was in control of the situation and intended to remain pure until they married.

Marriage? Well, Tim had not actually made any kind of commitment, but she felt in her heart that he soon would.

Their little kisses and touches became more involved, but they always quickly asked forgiveness of each other and God when the petting became intense. After several months of these heavy petting sessions, Susan began to feel Tim had become distant. She then began to think that she may not have adequately assured him of her love. Maybe he was having second thoughts about her. She feared she might lose him—but she couldn't! He was the one.

Susan purposed to do whatever it took to keep him. She wondered if she had acted old-fashioned. After all, she just knew they would marry one day. Maybe he just needed to know the depth of her commitment to him.

Gradually, their relationship became more and more physical until one evening, Susan gave Tim the gift she had vowed not to open until her honeymoon night. She had imagined how strong and pure this moment of

111

intimacy would make their love. Certainly this would cement the deep love they had for each other. It didn't.

Tim's face was no longer gentle. Susan felt as if he were a stranger. Her heart died within her. They were together, yet further apart than they had ever been. As he rose to leave, he said nothing. Instead of cementing their love, this one act of physical affection destroyed it. Susan longed to take her treasure back. She longed to start the night over. Unfortunately, the harsh reality had only just begun.

Tim and Susan are fictitious names, but this is a true story—and not just for this one young lady. It is true for hundreds of women who want to do what is right, but who unwisely give away their gift of physical purity too early. The gift is a treasure that can be rewrapped and given again, but never again for the first time.

Tim and Susan's story brings to mind a quote I have heard so many times: *"Men play at love to get sex, and women play at sex to get love."* Men get sex but the woman does not get love and commitment. My heart has broken for countless single gals who have *played at sex to get love,* but instead of love they are disposed of like a used paper cup.

LADY OF PURITY IN THE 21ST CENTURY

Someone might take a look at this section title and exclaim that it's an oxymoron, a completely unrealistic ideal! After all, it's impossible to be a Lady of Purity in such a sex-saturated society. If that were the case, then the biblical illustration of Boaz and Ruth would merely be a fairy tale, an idea that belongs only in a Disney cartoon. However, I wholeheartedly believe that a Lady of Purity can live and even thrive in the 21st century. Just as Ruth's purity allowed her to go to Boaz, request that he function as her kinsman redeemer, and exit his presence as pure as she entered, a Lady of Purity can sustain purity even in a context that greatly challenges her commitment to purity.

Before he left for college, a friend of our daughter's instigated a deeply intense conversation with her. He talked about the respect he had always maintained for her, a respect that he felt her "very being" demanded. He explained that he had not even tried to make a "move" on her because he so respected her purity.

What was so profound about this conversation was that the young man was not a follower of Jesus. When our daughter shared this with me, I was reminded again that a girl's purity is a heart guard, and more than that, it speaks loudly and clearly in the midst of this sex-saturated society.

This heart guard also protected our daughter when she was in college; it does so now, even *after* she is married. A woman's purity is, in fact, a lifelong guard of her heart (see 1 Cor. 6:19-20; Prov. 4:23).

A woman's purity is a lifelong guard of her heart.

We live in a day of blatant sexual impurity. A woman who marries, still a virgin, has become the exception, not the rule. Statistics say 80 percent of all unmarried women have given away their virginity by 20 years of age[1] The Ruth of our biblical story, like us, also lived in a society of rampant moral decay. Ruth's story occurs during a time of year when sexual promiscuity would be at its height in the small farming community of Israel: "Immoral practices at harvest times were by no means uncommon and, indeed appear to have been encouraged by the fertility rites practiced in some religions."[2]

In this promiscuous society Ruth was a Lady of Purity, even in the midst of a potentially compromising situation. Ruth 3:7 says:

> *When Boaz had eaten and drunk and his heart was merry, he went to lie down at the end of the heap of grain; and she came secretly, and uncovered his feet and lay down.*

At a glance, you may read this and picture the beginnings of an X-rated scene in Ruth's story. But you must realize that Ruth was acting according to the customs of the time. She was not slinking into Boaz's bed to seduce him.

In obedience to her mother-in-law's instructions, Ruth quietly lay at his feet for him to notice her, thus symbolizing her subjection to Boaz as her nearest of kin. This would give him the opportunity, if he so chose, to take legal action for the well-being of Ruth and her mother-in-law. (A woman had no form of social security and very few rights in that culture without a man.) This was not a brazen act of seduction, but an act of obedience to God's plan for her provision in that day. One thing is certain. When she left to go home, she walked away as a Lady of Purity.

Although the customs of Ruth's day may be difficult to understand, the temptations to compromise physically are not. Unfortunately, many women have been snared by the devil's deceptions and robbed of their innocence. How does today's single woman safeguard this special treasure and, like Ruth, go home at night a Lady of Purity?

DEADLY DECEPTION

Remember how the serpent deceived Eve by causing her to question God? He caused her to believe that God wanted to deny her something good, not provide her with something better. The enemy wants you to believe that if you wait to have sex, you will miss out on some of the delights of life.

Godly women must avoid basing their comprehension of the pleasures of sex on what commercials advertise, magazines glamorize, or books sensationalize. These are all full of the enemy's propaganda. Today's society seeks ultimate pleasure with no pain. But following society's example usually brings just the opposite. Look to your heavenly Father, your Creator, for the truth. God gives true sexual fulfillment to the lady who waits for this gift. God intended for you to enjoy the fulfillment and pleasure of sex within marriage only. The wonder and joy of this intimate act is maximized through purity before marriage.

Ask any woman of God who waited and she will tell you with eyes aglow that it was worth the sacrifice of denying her desires for a time. Look at that woman's marriage. Most likely the romance between her and her spouse still burns in a delightful love affair. Compare this real-life situation to the illusions in just one half-hour of "true life" romance on the television in an episode of

"As the Stomach Turns" or "Body Watch." Have those actresses and actors (who, by the way, never scrub a toilet or break a nail and who always seem to be in their evening gown attire) found true fulfillment? They shout, "Ah! Yes—the delights of sex." Do not be deceived. Sex is special! Not sensuous sex, but satisfying sex in your Creator's way and time.

WHY WAIT?

Since sex is desirable, why not have sex? Why would God want to limit your pleasure with someone for whom you feel affection but haven't married? Have you ever been dieting but treated yourself to a huge piece of rich chocolate cake with fudge icing to celebrate some special occasion? Cake is good. Cake is desirable. The more cake, the more pleasure. But cake, in the midst of a strict diet, can really make one sick! The pleasure of a big, luscious piece of cake depends on the right timing, just as the pleasures of sex do.

God wants you to be a Lady of Purity because He wants to protect you from the consequences that sex before marriage brings. These consequences can be physical, emotional, relational, and spiritual.

God wants you to be a Lady of Purity because He wants to protect you from the consequences that sex before marriage brings. These consequences can be physical, emotional, relational, and spiritual. Let's look at these a little more closely.

PHYSICAL IMPACT OF SEXUAL PROMISCUITY

Have you ever secretly opened a Christmas gift before Christmas Day and rewrapped it, putting it back under the tree? How thrilling and exciting it was when you saw the surprise. But what about the "big day" when the gifts were supposed to be opened for the first time? Where was the excitement when you opened your gift? The gift did not seem quite as special because it had already been opened for the first time.

Each woman receives one "first time." God desires for your precious gift to be given to a committed lover who will cherish, keep, and protect you in marriage. God wants you and your gift to this man to be treasured and cherished, not trampled and conquered. Song of Solomon 8:4 (NIV) says, *"Do not arouse or awaken love until it so desires."* God wants to protect you from losing your virginity.

God also wants to protect you from the sexually transmitted diseases that could affect not only you, but also your future husband. One young single cried the night she discovered that she had contracted genital warts. She grieved over the realization that when her future knight in shining armor proposed to her, she would have to disclose the fact that she carried an infectious disease. This grieved her more than the fact that genital warts are incurable. Not only could you or your husband personally incur irreparable physical damage, but also transmit these infectious diseases to your future children.

God also desires to shield you from an unwanted pregnancy. Although precautions exist, pregnancy always remains a possibility. A rushed marriage, adoption, or abortion only complicates the consequences.

Judy, a wonderful Christian girl with a promising future, looked forward to graduating from high school. To celebrate this special occasion, she went to a party with a great-looking guy. She decided a few drinks that night would be okay. She didn't want to seem "different" in front of her date. His invitation to go off to a secluded room made her feel uncomfortable, but the evening was so special and her date was so kind and tender and romantic.

In the following months, Judy tried to deny the physical changes she was experiencing. Bible college would start soon, so she blamed them on the stress. God had forgiven her for going all the way that night—surely He would not have allowed her to get pregnant. It would ruin all her plans.

Only after her mother noticed her condition did Judy go for a doctor's appointment. Unfortunately, it confirmed the worst of her fears. Judy would soon be a mother. Regardless of how sorry she was and the fact that God had forgiven her, the consequences of that one act changed her life forever. God wanted to protect Judy physically, but He left the choices up to her.

God desires to shield you from the negative physical consequences of premarital sex. He wants to protect you from sinning against your body. First Corinthians 6:18 (NIV) says, *"Flee from sexual immorality. All other sins a [woman] commits are outside [her] body, but [she] who sins sexually sins against [her] own body."* "He wants you to be free from an addiction to premarital sex. Passionate physical exchange is a short-lived high. As with drugs, you keep wanting more intense highs."[3]

THE LAW OF DIMINISHING RETURNS

Do you remember the first time you went somewhere you were just *so* excited about—maybe an amusement park as a kid or a particular restaurant as an adult? All your senses were heightened to take in the experience in as many ways as you could. And it was fabulous! The colors were saturated, the rides were a thrill, the food was incomparably delicious. Now you have gone again... and again. And while you might still enjoy that roller coaster or appreciate the familiar taste of that particular molten chocolate cake, it's not what you would call a thrill anymore.

These are examples of the law of diminishing returns. The return you get from your experience gets less profound or less intense over time.

Certainly you can see how this principle would apply to the challenge of remaining sexually pure. The law of diminishing returns in relation to sex begins with this simple statement: There is no such thing as a non-stimulating caress or kiss. Such affection may seem innocent, but it is rare that it remains innocent. After several sessions of kissing for an extended period of time, the brain-chemical high diminishes, and the couple needs to do something else to attain a comparable high. After all, God made the human body sexual for a particular progression—one that is meant to be followed to its end in the context of marriage. So that very chemistry He wired us with is *designed* to yearn for more.

SEXUAL BRINKMANSHIP

Because of how we are created, for all people, Christian or not, there is a natural progression toward sexual fulfillment. That fulfillment pursued outside of marriage, however, is sin. A couple pushes the limits all the way to the edge—to the brink—and then finds they have gone much too far. This sexual brinkmanship begins with what one assumes is cute and innocent and ends up destroying the relationship.

Sexual brinkmanship begins with what one assumes is cute and innocent and ends up destroying the relationship.

The following is a list that people move through because of the law of diminishing returns. And let me reiterate, this sexual brinkmanship has no regard for the Christian or non-Christian.

Natural Progression toward Sexual Sin:

1. Look

2. Touch

3. Holding hands lightly

4. Holding hands constantly

5. Light kiss

6. Strong kissing

7. French kissing (entering the No Zone—below the neck—prep for intercourse)

8. Fondling breasts

9. Fondling organs

10. Sexual intercourse

When you consider the law of diminishing returns within the context of a sex-saturated society, even a Lady of Purity can move from #1 to #10 faster than she would dream—and in this case, that dream can become a nightmare!

The following is how I illustrate this law when warning parents and teens about what looks innocent. This same warning needs to be considered by every Lady of Purity who wants to guard her heart and body. And take note! Being an older single does not eliminate the need to consider the reality of the law of diminishing returns.

Let me illustrate this law and how it might play out for a teen (though, once again, there is no age limit on these truths!). You go to the mall with some girlfriends—or at least that's what you tell your parents. Maybe the guy you are crushing on invited you to meet him at the mall. You know that your parents feel safe when you're at the mall, in public—what's the big deal who you're meeting there? But let's be honest: malls and movies are *exactly* where young people have ample opportunity to move through the list.

Even if your mom and dad do know you are meeting a boy there, you're just going to "walk around the mall together." So, as you're strolling around, this boy who already has your complete attention takes your hand. As sweet and innocent as this act of affection may seem, it is very easy to be unprepared for the potent physical effect of that first touch. The thrill of this special guy holding your hand can only be compared to a trip to Disney World—fireworks over Cinderella's Castle! I mean, you have an emotional heart attack; you feel electricity flow up your arm the moment he takes your hand in his.

Imagine in our scenario that you have to leave the mall—and the guy—because someone is picking you up. You walk away from him, giddy as a little girl on Christmas morning. You keep saying to yourself, "I can't believe he held my hand!" In fact, you're so excited, you manage to text ten friends before you get to the car! Ten times you repeat your delightful experience (if you are *female*, you *know* I am not exaggerating): "We were looking in the window at Petco. It was *sooo* sweet! There were the cutest little puppies and he just reached over and took my hand!"

Now you may be smiling at this last sentence, but the reality of the law of diminishing returns has already set in. (I vividly remember where I was when my husband held my hand for the first time—Six Flags Over Georgia during our last ride together in the park before heading back to our college campus!)

Let's continue the journey to sexual brinkmanship. When you see this young man again—let's say at youth group—he will take your hand the minute you sit down. This time, although you're happy, the fireworks over Cinderella's Castle do not happen. You might assume that the fireworks are stifled by the atmosphere of the youth meeting. Sitting there, you are already planning how to duplicate the *previous* experience by returning to the mall. So, the next week, you make a plan to meet him at the mall again, and if you "have to," you even lie to your parents about who's going to be there. (It's a big, red flag, ladies, if you find yourself lying to family or friends about meeting a certain guy! Bozo guys often require the girl to lie to arrange to be alone together.)

So you get to the mall and you spot Mr. Wonderful. He takes your hand and you begin to wander around. Yet you are absolutely shocked! When he touches your hand there are no fireworks, no electricity. You wonder, "Is this the same hand?" You even look down at his hand as you ponder the dilemma! Where did the thrill go? Do I not like him anymore? Maybe we need to walk down to the pet store where he *first* held my hand; maybe seeing those cute puppies will help the thrill return with the memory.

STRIVING FOR THE CHEMISTRY HIGH

You may have already had this experience, so you know what comes next: you leave the mall that day completely puzzled. What you don't know is that *with physical touch you are always progressing toward a more potent physical thrill.* So the next time you meet this guy at the mall, he puts his arm around your shoulders, pulling you closer to his side, and—guess what?—the fireworks return! Woot-Woot! You are excited and, frankly, relieved. You are convinced that your love is here to stay.

Now it's routine. You are a couple.

When you walk around, you hold hands, and at the youth meeting he always puts his arm around you. You are elated for this physical display of admiration from your boyfriend in front of all your peers (which your parents may or may not know about at all). You may not realize it, but you are getting ready for a move toward the No Zone that is inevitable after his next move.

The next step is utterly predictable, as you begin to wonder when he will finally kiss you (thoughts that are almost always egged on by girlfriends, sisters, or even mothers!). He "finally" kisses you and the fireworks return; and if that is where it stopped, no parent would have to fear an "innocent little kiss." But the problem is that no kiss is innocent and no kiss is non-stimulating. The next time he kisses you it doesn't have that thrill unless the kissing time is extended. Then kissing isn't as thrilling, so a little tongue is added.

Can you see how easily this all progresses toward doing more than you ever intended to do? You don't understand that you are actually *marching* toward the No Zone with careless disregard as you engage in activities that deliver you to the sexual brink, and inevitably intercourse.

The fundamental problem is this: most teens have only *heard* that they should not have sex before marriage. Their youth leaders and parents have all said to wait until marriage for sex; but they have rarely had the law of diminishing returns explained to them. They have simply been told "Wait," without explaining how or *why*.

Too many gals—young and older—don't understand that when you go to the No Zone (area below the neck), you are going too far. That zone was made to be traversed in marriage. Years ago while I was teaching this at Liberty University to a group of students, my daughter was in the back listening. She responded to me later, "I know I used to tease you about it, Mom, but please, you have to warn people. They don't get this."

I know they don't.

QUICKER SEXUAL BRINK IN THE NEXT RELATIONSHIP

Something even more terrifying than this slippery slope within a relationship is the reality that when gals and guys date and break up—*the next relationship has a built-in accelerator because of previous fooling around.* When a girl breaks up with a guy because they fell over the sexual brink, the next time she starts dating, the law of diminishing returns almost guarantees her moving faster through the various levels of physical expression. After all, she has already diminished the thrill by going too far in the last relationship, and the chemistry will not be as satisfying on the more "innocent" levels of communicating physically! Consequently you can go from simple handholding to aggressive kissing—or even more—in only one date.

DRAWING THE LINE: REMEMBER THE NO ZONE

Even the nicest girl you know cannot participate in the behavior on our list and not end up going further than her heart would guide her. God created the No Zone for marriage. Gals all around the world think they can play around and exercise fierce self-control as they reach the end of the list: #10 Sexual Intercourse. Here are some sobering statistics that indicate the *younger* a girl starts to date, the *more likely* she is to be sexually active before marriage:

Girls Dating by Age—Intercourse Pre-marriage

- 12-year-olds: 91 percent

- 13-year-olds: 56 percent

- 14-year-olds: 53 percent

- 15-year-olds: 40 percent

- 16-year-olds: 20 percent

Teens need time to develop their self-control muscles. There have been lots of references over the past few years about the latest research on the development of the brain's frontal cortex. It has been shown that this part of the brain monitors impulse control, but does not fully develop until a person is in his or her mid-twenties. Too many times at mother-daughter events, I meet junior high girls who are already dating and I want to scream, "Do you not have a mother? Is your mother at this event with you?"

Why is it that we have security systems on our homes and totally miss the security system our girls need—boundaries on their emotional craziness! Letting a pubescent, hormonally driven girl go on dates and get into relationships before she is sixteen (and even sixteen is too young for some) is the ultimate insanity.

When our children were teens, they didn't go anywhere unless they were in a group. We would joke and call it "international date night," because the kids were all ages and always traveled in a mob. There was an unwritten rule they all seemed to abide by: no pairing up! What is so great is that by staying in a group and getting to know so many kids, these former teens remain friends today—and they are all in their thirties.

WHY DO CHRISTIANS GO TOO FAR?

We may not be at all shocked by what goes on in the culture at large. But we have to wake up and be very attentive to the situation in our youth groups and Christian schools. Why are our precious kids acting just like teens in the world? Why are Christian kids getting pregnant? I found an old note that was written at a teen conference in early 2000 that stated: "Forty-three percent of kids from fundamental churches have had sex by nineteen years old." In a 2011 report, according to some research, that percentage has risen to more like 80 percent!

I have three straightforward replies to my questions in the previous paragraph:

1. They get pregnant because they *didn't plan on going all the way!*

2. They are dating too young.

3. They have not developed the muscle of sexual self-control.

Scripture is clear *"…*[a girl] *is a slave to whatever has mastered* [her]*"* (see 2 Pet. 2:19 NIV).

CRITICAL REASON TO WAIT

One of the most critical reasons not to have sex before marriage is the emotionally blinding impact of sex on any dating relationship. This blinding reality is a natural consequence that is *built in by God.* God's will concerning sex before marriage is spelled out in crystal clarity in First Thessalonians 4:3-5 (NIV):

> *It is God's will that you should be sanctified: that you should avoid sexual immorality; that each of you should learn to control his own body in a way that is holy and honorable, not in passionate lust like the heathen, who do not know God.*

This is the will of God: that you abstain from sexual immorality. Bam! Purity is the will of God. No one has to debate it with the youth pastor. It is God's will, no exceptions. And we parents can yell "Amen!" to our heavenly Father's guidelines—*abstain.*

**One of the most critical reasons not to have sex
before marriage is the emotionally blinding impact
of sex on any dating relationship.**

What a Lady of Purity needs to grasp is that God clearly designed sex for marriage. You need to know that the violation of this boundary on sex blinds you to the context of the Bozo guys you are so "in love with."

This simple concept that *sex ruins a good relationship or sustains a bad one* should be on a Post-it Note on your bathroom mirror while prepping for a date. Right now you may know a gal who is dating a guy who is not good for her. In fact, you have watched him be rude to this friend, and you are confused as to why she would even date such a Bozo. You may find yourself thinking, "Why would she be with him? I'd never let a guy talk to me like that."

The unfortunate reality of the *why* behind a precious gal dating such a Bozo guy is too often this: she has become involved physically with her boyfriend. When a gal allows a guy to move to the No Zone, the bodily involvement becomes like a "hood" over her head, and she can no longer see clearly what a Bozo she is dating. Everyone around her can see it, but she is blinded—and actually trapped—by the hood that she's pulled over her own head!

EMOTIONAL IMPACT OF SEXUAL PROMISCUITY

God intricately and delicately formed women with emotional characteristics that differ from men. Women's emotional and physical states are woven closely together. Those of us who struggle with PMS know how difficult it can be to separate what's going on in our physical body from our emotional state.

Well, consider that the man who touches your body also touches your emotions. God made you that way, and He desires to protect your heart from being ripped apart by any man. You cannot make love to a man and remain emotionally untouched, no matter how hard you try. Therefore, if God knows that the man you think you love cannot care for your heart, He does not want you to give him any part of your body. You cannot give one without affecting the other! Your heavenly Father longs to keep your emotions safe and to guard you from feelings that threaten to wreck your emotional well-being!

God wants to protect you from the devastation of condemnation. The devil loves to get you down, to make you feel unworthy, thus making you unable to glorify God or stand before others. He enhances this tactic when he can whisper in your ear, "Some Christian you are. How can you witness to Jane? She may have heard…. You can't be a missionary; you compromised, remember?" Condemned…condemned…condemned.

If your emotions lied to you, causing you to give away your treasure to the wrong man, haunting fears may also begin to plague you: *Will he still respect me? Will he still love me? Why is that all he wants from me right now? What if I'm pregnant? Will anyone else find out? What if my parents find out? How can I face them? If we break up, what if the next man I date finds out?* Day and night these fears can play on your mind and emotions. God wants to protect you from these emotional traumas.

After premarital sex, there will usually be some lurking doubts. *Would he have loved me without my body? Would he have married me if I hadn't gotten pregnant? Will he be attracted to someone better looking after we're married?* Most overwhelming are the doubts of God's love for you and, possibly, doubts of your salvation or your ability to ever again have a morally pure relationship.

You can be fully forgiven and cleansed by Christ, but damaged emotions take time to heal. The Lord doesn't want you to suffer these hurts. You are precious to Him. That's why He sets loving limits on your physical relationship and emotional attachments.

The emotional burdens of condemnation, fear, and doubt are often compounded with many other emotions such as resentment, bitterness, depression, and mistrust. God created you with emotions that can be overwhelmed by sexual promiscuity. Let Him protect your heart.

RELATIONAL IMPACT OF SEXUAL PROMISCUITY

A woman has a depth of soul that desires an intimate friendship, apart from anything physical, with the man she loves. She desires to be known for the woman she is, not just for her physical body. A couple who chooses to remain physically pure gives all their time and attention to knowing one another on a deeper mental and emotional level. Once passion is introduced into the relationship, it is difficult for the man to stop and be satisfied again with just developing the friendship. The man becomes distracted by the physical. This is why so many women enjoy the relationship until the "friendship" changes to "dating." Something is lost when physical passion begins.

You cannot give double messages. Either you want him to know the you on the inside or the you on the outside. If you encourage your date to play with the bow on your package, he will want to untie the ribbon and unwrap the gift. Don't distract him with the bow. Allowing sex to enter into a relationship before marriage will almost always result in the loss of an intimate friendship with the one you desire to know you for you.

Premarital sex also brings a consequence that remains hidden until you marry. Mistrust and disrespect surface after the wedding cake has been eaten and "postmarital insecurity" begins. When a couple becomes involved sexually before marriage, they massage their consciences with the rationalization that they will marry anyway, so their lack of self-control doesn't matter. This is where they are wrong! Lack of self-control before marriage is *fornication*. Lack of self-control after marriage is *adultery*. The seeds for adultery are planted in the "hotbeds" of fornication. A woman subconsciously wonders, "If he did not exhibit self-control with me before marriage, how can I be sure that he will not give in to temptation during marriage when an attractive younger woman comes along?" A young man who cannot control himself before marriage does not suddenly become a man of self-control because he wears a wedding band!

Two other very real relational consequences deal with your present and future families. Think of your parents' shame about your sexual choices. Also, what about your future children? One day you may face your children knowing that you did not set an example of purity for them to follow. What will you say if they ask the question, "Did you and Dad wait?"

Finally, if you do not marry the man who opened your gift first, you take memories of him into your marriage that flash back to haunt you. God wants you to have the joy of saying to your knight on that special wedding night, "Here I am, clean and pure, emotionally and physically. No one has touched the treasure of my love. I kept myself for you."

**God intended man and woman to enjoy a love
that the physical relationship merely enhances.**

God knows that a woman has much more to offer than a body. He knows that the dynamic relationship a woman has with a man is more than a physical experience. God intended man and woman to enjoy not merely sexual intercourse, but a love that the physical relationship merely enhances. This love remains even when there is no physical culmination. Sometimes physical contact distracts a couple from developing and enjoying communication. If you want the friendship to be knowing who you each are, don't distract each other with early or inappropriate physical contact.

SEX RUINS A GOOD RELATIONSHIP

How does sex ruin a good relationship? When two people start dating and become involved physically, the innocence disappears and one of their consciences will likely shout—"Get out!"

When I first became a Christian, and had newly left behind a sex-saturated dating mentality, I started dating this wonderful Christian guy. His commitment to moral purity touched my heart profoundly. After dating for a year, this young man's moral purity was challenged by a young woman—*me!*

I had assumed the inevitability of moving toward the sexual brink, especially since we were talking about a future life together. I only understood a dating world where sexual sin was actually one of the requirements. When this godly young man broke up with me, I was absolutely devastated. After recovering from the shock, the Lord very kindly brought to my mind a night when this young man and I went too far. We went to the No Zone for a moment—but the moment ended our relationship!

Spiritual passion makes it difficult to see that God also set physical limits to protect you spiritually. Hebrews 13:4 (NIV) very clearly says that *"Marriage should be honored by all, and the marriage bed kept pure, for God will judge the adulterer and all the sexually immoral."* God judges the sin of immorality. It feels awful to be separated from your Lord by the guilt of sin.

Actions speak louder than words, and this is especially true regarding premarital sex. It is difficult to share Christ with one who knows your reputation. Your actions can also cause weaker brothers and sisters to stumble. One night of passion can totally destroy a reputation you have built over a lifetime.

The spiritual side of sex is often overlooked. Even many Christians are not aware of the profoundly spiritual nature of their sex lives. A person will feel acute spiritual pain and separation from God when engaging in sex outside of marriage, but may not even realize how spiritually beneficial and unifying sex is within marriage.[4]

God does not intend to deny you pleasure. He protects you so you might enjoy physical health, emotional stability, relational intimacy, and spiritual blessings. If you marry, He wants you to grow more in love with your husband with each passing year. He wants you to live in complete trust of one another and spend a lifetime in love instead of the consequences of a fleeting night of uncontrolled lust.

THE GIFT OF NO

No is a gift you give to a man you care about, just as his respect for your response is a gift to you. In his book *To Own a Dragon*, Don Miller validates my remarks: "Women saying no to men, not letting men have sex with them, causes men to step up…. I think men need women to be women, and we need to be made to jump through some hoops. If a woman withholds sex until she gets what she wants, we are all better for it."[5] A gal is actually blessing her guy when she says no. She is enhancing his inner world and strengthening his potential to leave his adolescence.

So to help with the civilizing of men, stop cheering for the Bozo tribe. Stop validating their distorted view of sex by compromising your moral ideals.

I have a friend who didn't want to wear the typical purity ring. She wanted something trendier than a ring symbolic of her keeping her virginity until she got married. What did she do? She had her belly button pierced with a blue gemstone. The blue stone was because of the "blue cord" that was to be a reminder to obey.

> *Throughout the generations to come you are to make tassels on the corners of your garments with a blue cord on each tassel. You will have these tassels to look at and so you will remember all the commands of the Lord, that you may obey them and not prostitute yourselves by going after the lusts of your own hearts and eyes* (Numbers 15:38-39 NIV).

Even before a couple starts to date seriously, the guy needs to practice saying no to Miss Lust so that he can resist her tempting voice after the wedding day.

Every time a woman says no, she is cheering on a man's capacity to control his own body in honor for God's glory.

Again, for a woman, young or old, the sobering power of no is the greatest gift she can give to her a man. Every time she says no, she is cheering on his capacity to control his own body in honor for God's glory. Every time she says no, she is helping a Boaz stay strong, or she is refusing to be Bozo bait for someone who will use her, then move on.[6]

Guarding the Treasure

How then does a Lady in Waiting guard her purity? Once a man has a woman's heart, her body is not far behind. That is one reason Proverbs 4:23 says, *"Watch over your heart with all diligence, for from it flow the springs of life."* To walk in purity, a Lady in Waiting must first guard the key to her heart. This does not imply that your relationships with men are robotic and free from feelings. It means that you focus on growing in friendship, not romance.

Here is how Debby guarded her purity while dating:

I asked the Lord to help me remember not to take my heart away from Him and give it to a boyfriend too quickly. To keep this commitment, I decided I would pray before accepting any date. Before going out, I would pray again, this time asking that my thoughts and actions during the time together would not center on encouraging him romantically, but building a friendship and encouraging his love for the Lord. At times, when I felt flutters of romance rising and my heart trembling, I would ask the Lord to renew my strength and reset my focus; I would picture myself kneeling in new commitment.

I enjoyed friendship-building "dating" more after deciding to let God protect my heart. The only man who was given the key to my heart was the man I married. When we were engaged, I gave him a small red velvet box with an antique key inside to symbolize that I was giving him my heart to care for and cherish as the Lord had done before I met him. I am grateful that now Bill cherishes me as a priceless treasure and views the key to my heart as a privileged possession. An added bonus is that marriage is full of the "extra special" romances that I denied myself before I met my husband.

Don't let your heart be given away too easily. If a man says he loves you, you don't have to echo the phrase. To men these three words can mean all kinds of things, like "I lust for you," or "I want you to kiss me." Or maybe he just can't think of anything else to say at the moment! But what did that "I love you" do to your heartstrings? Gradually those "I love yous" can trap you emotionally and lead you on physically. To guard the key to your heart, make a commitment to say you love someone only if you love him with a committed love, not a casual love feeling. You will remain much more in control of your friendship.

Real love will have time to blossom and grow without those three words. Guard and save them to be whispered when God reveals it is time. What a gift to tell your fiancé, "You are the first person I have ever said this to: 'I love you.'" Give meaning to those precious words, and you may use them and hear them with fondness through many happy years of marriage.

There's a second step you can take to guard your purity. It's a radical statement, but *save all your kisses for your future husband.* One woman who made this decision said, "Early in my dating, I tired of giving a kiss at the door for a hamburger, coke, and fries. What would I have to give next for a steak dinner or a night on the town? After I was married, I realized the decision not to give my kisses freely to my dates had an added bonus. For every kiss I denied dates at the door, the man I married received my kisses 'with interest' in our years of marriage. It was worth waiting for kisses—so they would be full of meaning—for years."

A woman's kiss or embrace is not just another way of saying thank you! A kiss should say something more intimate. If so, do you want to say intimate things to every guy you date? All the kisses you give before marriage and all the kisses you give after marriage express the love that belongs to one person: your knight.

If you remember to whom your kisses belong, you won't be so quick to give them away. If you think you may be dating Mr. Right, give your friendship time to grow before you give the "fringe benefits." He will appreciate them and respect you much more if you wait.

Realize that a kiss starts physical contact and once you get started it's hard to turn back from passion. Determine what you mean with a kiss. Let it reveal your heart, not "rev up" your hormones. One lady put it this way when asked why "friends" have trouble becoming friends again once they start dating: "Once you start having sex, that's about the only thing you have in common."

Decide what you will and will not do with a date before things become hot and heavy.

A third practical step is to make your decisions and choices about what you will and will not do with a date *before* things become hot and heavy. Here are some examples of "dating standards" that many godly women have made. They will help you resist the pressure to "open the gift" too early. (You can find more in Chapter 9.)

- I will date only growing Christian men. (You will most likely marry a man you date. This is important!)

- I will concentrate on the friendship—not romance. (Don't be tricked!)

- I will not spend time with him at home when we are alone.

- I will not give kisses and hugs freely.

- I will not lie down beside a man.

Don't set standards "as you go." Emotions can be tricky. You must make wise choices before the "flutters" and "heartthrobs" become so loud you cannot hear yourself think. Write them down and read them often! Commit them to God regularly in prayer.

During a Bible study, one Lady in Waiting made this point about "dating":

Before Jesus became Lord of my relationships, I accepted our society's idea of dating as the time for a man and woman to be alone together. This time usually was devoted to romance and involved a measure of physical involvement—gradually accelerating if the dating continued. As I became closer to the Lord, I began to see dating from His perspective as a time for friendship-building without a need for promises of love or giving physical affection. As I spend time in group situations instead of one-to-one dating, I can really see the character of the guy friends I am spending time with. Doing things with groups also guards our purity, but doesn't limit our friendship-building and communication. When I do spend time with a guy, I don't refer to it as dating any longer. I talk about "friendship-building" founded on Christ—the One who holds my heart and guides the friendship.

Too many women think that if they give a man what he is longing for in terms of physical satisfaction, they will inevitably win his love forever. Hundreds of women have lowered their standards sexually and gone further than they knew the Lord wanted in hopes of hanging on to the guy they were spending time with. It's a lie. Don't believe it!

Women are easily turned on by words. Most men know this. Another way to protect your purity is to stand on guard when you hear "sweet talk." Don't let any of these lines cause you to surrender:

- If you love me…

- I have never felt such love before…

- Just try it once…

- I won't get you pregnant…

- I want to spend the rest of my life with you…

- Since we're going to be married anyway…

- Nobody is still a virgin at your age…

- What we do in private is no one else's business…

- If we only go so far and not all the way, it's OK…

- They are doing it, and they are Christians…

- If you won't prove your love, I'll find someone who will…

- You are too old-fashioned…

- Do it now so we will be prepared for marriage…

- It will never happen to us…

You can't believe any of these lines. They have been said before, the gift has been opened, and the lady left in an emotional heap labeled "conquered." These words have trapped many ladies—beware! When you catch yourself rationalizing what you are doing and assuring yourself you are in control, make a second check. You'll be glad you did. A godly man will not pressure a woman verbally, but will cherish her with his declarations of love and take her home before they have to regret any violation of their purity.

WHAT WOMEN DON'T COMPREHEND

It doesn't matter how much education a woman has or doesn't have, this idea seems to elude most of them: a man who does not succeed in keeping his sexual urges under God's control before marriage will not be successful controlling his improper sexual urges after marriage. Thus "sexual and holy" is an essential element of a man worth waiting for. It is a dangerous principle not to grasp. Premarital sex is a postdated check for postmarital unfaithfulness!

Premarital sex is a postdated check for postmarital unfaithfulness!

What too many women misunderstand is that sexual temptation does not subside with marriage but actually increases in a different context. As mentioned previously, violating sexual boundaries before marriage is called *fornication*, and violating sexual boundaries after marriage is called *adultery*. The key for postmarital faithfulness is the premarital prep of self-control![7]

WHAT IF IT'S TOO LATE?

You do not have to make the same mistakes many have made. But if you are reading this "after the fact" and are dealing with the guilt of the lost gift, do not be discouraged. Although it is true that there is only one first time, God is the God of the first-time experience. Let Him heal your broken heart through forgiveness. Agree with God that you have sinned and leave the sin before Him. Then guard yourself from entering into that sin pattern again. Learn a valuable lesson, but do not continue to beat yourself with condemnation.

As a teenager, I wholeheartedly embraced forgiveness for my sexual impurity and received from Jesus the gift of secondary virginity. By God's grace, I developed sexual self-control that protected me before marriage and throughout four decades of marriage. Jesus paid for those sins at Calvary. Do not continue to allow yourself or the enemy to defeat you (see Rev.12:10-11) with remembering a sin once you have confessed it to God and those you have offended. There may be consequences of your sin, but you do not have to live with the guilt of it.

God is the God who forgives and forgets. Jeremiah 31:34 says, *"...for I will forgive their iniquity, and their sin I will remember no more."* One of God's greatest abilities is that He forgets the sins of those who belong to Christ Jesus, *"I, even I, am the One who wipes out your transgressions for My own sake; and I will not remember your sins"* (Isa. 43:25). Let this be your motto:

> *...but one thing I do: forgetting what lies behind* [as God does] *and reaching forward to what lies ahead, I press on toward the goal for the prize of the upward call of God in Christ Jesus* (Philippians 3:13-14).

Even though you have been freed from the guilt by confession, do not use it as an opportunity to continue in sin or to leave yourself open to temptation. Continue to choose freedom over sin's mastery. Lay aside every encumbrance and the sin that so easily entangles you and run with endurance the race set before you (see Heb. 12:1). How? Fix your eyes on Jesus (not on your sin, the past, or even yourself). Jesus is the Author and Perfecter of your faith (see Heb. 12:2).

There is one last response that brings complete freedom. You must forgive and forget the sins of those who sinned against you. Jesus is very clear in Matthew 5:21-24 about what to do with anger toward a brother. But how do you do it? First choose to forgive your brother with your heart, and then God will help you work through the emotions that may remain. You will not be free of the hurt if you harbor bitterness. A quick way to ruin a beautiful complexion is to hold on to an unforgiving, bitter attitude.

If you have opened your gift too soon, do not be kept from beginning new again. Accept God's forgiveness and refuse to feel like damaged goods. God has better in store for you. You, dear Lady in Waiting, are a treasure. The enemy attempts to deceive you when he offers to delight you by his ways and means. Don't lose sight of the value of what you have or of who you are. Don't allow the flickering pleasures of an evening of "making love" destroy a lifetime of "lasting love."

BECOMING A LADY OF PURITY

- Second Samuel 13:1-19 is a painful story of rape, but note the reaction of the man who got what he wanted. After his sexual thirst was quenched, what was his response toward the woman for whom he lusted? How did he feel toward the woman? Why?

- How can a young woman stay pure? (See Psalm 119:9,11.)

- How do friendships affect your purity? (See First Corinthians 15:33.)

- Write out a specific list of ways you will guard your purity as you build relationships with the opposite sex.

- Discuss the Law of Diminishing Returns.

- Is striving to be pure too hard? (See First Corinthians 10:13.) List some of the ways of escape God has given you.

- Consider the statement that "sex ruins a good relationship or sustains a bad one." Discuss how sex can "blind" the dating couple and the built-in consequences it brings! (See Galatians 6:7-8.)

- Do you have a friend who is dating a Bozo and clearly cannot see him for who he really is? (Pray for her eyes to be opened.)

- At What Price the Dream? Discuss the Consequences of Pre-marital Sex (#8 is the *worst!).*

1. Suspicion: Am I the only one he has ever done this with?

2. Guilt: A heavy heart of guilt because you are guilty of violating God's design.

3. Fear: What happens if I get pregnant? What if I get an STD? (Note: If guys got the STDs they give to girls, they might develop stronger self-control muscles. Guys spread genital herpes, but they are not impacted by them as profoundly as girls are.)

4. Communication breakdown: Petting begins, and the talking ends. Communication is a key to a good marriage. Exploring each other's body without exploring each other's soul (through communication) is a disaster in the making.

5. Respect/loss of trust: If I can't trust him to exercise self-control before marriage, I can't trust his sexual self-control after marriage.

6. Deception: Being deceived into thinking you're in love, but sex is not love. Eros is blinding.

7. Unfair comparisons: Sex causes you to compare one person with another (damaging memories on file).

8. Post-marital insecurity: Unfaithful husbands were lacking in sexual self-control before marriage. King David never saw the enormous price tag on the back of naked Bathsheba. The presence of physical involvement deceives a person into thinking that he or she is "in love."

   • Write out what a kiss means to you. What are you wanting to say when you kiss a man? Is there any other way to say this? How could adding physical affection to a friendship limit communication-building?

ENDNOTES

1. Nadine Joseph, "The New Rules of Courtship," *Newsweek* Magazine, Special Edition, Summer/Fall (1990), 27.

2. Arthur E. Cundall and Leon Morris, *Judges and Ruth, an Introduction and Commentary* (Chicago, IL: InterVarsity Press, 1968), 287.

3. Tim Stanford, "The Best of Sex," *Campus Life Magazine* (February 1992), 25–26.

4. Ibid.

5. Don Miller, *To Own a Dragon* (Colorado Springs, CO: NavPress Publishing Group, 2006).

6. Jackie Kendall, *A Man Worth Waiting For* (Nashville, TN: Faith Words, 2008), 194.

7. Ibid., 86.

Chapter 7

LADY OF SECURITY

"I still can't believe it!" one friend exclaimed. "I had a date with the perfect guy! I spent days searching for and finding a gorgeous outfit, I had my nails done, and my hair looked better than it ever has. I took a whole day off work to get ready and left in plenty of time to get there. The 150-mile drive to pick him up was nothing. I could have flown I was so excited. I tried to calm myself down the whole drive, but could not help thinking how right we were for each other, how beautiful our relationship and future would be. We went to a very romantic setting. I can't believe it! I was ready, willing, available. Everything was perfect, except for one problem. It turned out that he was gay."

This single woman diligently and faithfully "went after her man," only to find disappointment and pain. Ruth, our epitome of a Lady in Waiting, had a totally different approach.

Then he [Boaz] said, "May you be blessed of the Lord, my daughter. You have shown your last kindness to be better than the first by not going after young men, whether poor or rich. Now, my daughter, do not fear. I will do for you whatever you ask, for all my people in the city know that you are a woman of excellence" (Ruth 3:10-11).

Ruth—single, young, and widowed—must have experienced the lonely longings for the warmth of a husband. But she lived in victory over the desire to "man hunt." Instead of "going after the boys," she sat still and let God bring her prince to her. She was a Lady of Security.

FEELINGS OF INSECURITY

Why do women tend to "go after the guys"? Why do women experience difficulty being still and waiting for the man to initiate and develop the relationship? You find the answer in one word: insecurity. An insecure woman has her world centered on something (marriage) or someone (Mr. Right) that can be lost or taken away. Insecurity keeps a woman from experiencing consistent joy even within a relationship because a man cannot provide security, only God can.

**An insecure woman has her world centered
on something (marriage) or someone (Mr. Right)
that can be lost or taken away.**

Insecurity causes you to cling to a relationship. You feel a lack of confidence unless you have a man. When he is not with you, you fear he will not come back or call again. You want him to make a commitment so you will not lose him. You want all his time and attention. All your dreams, plans, and goals revolve around him. Insecurity in a relationship can cause jealousy and bickering. It makes you lose your confidence when he looks at another woman. You want to know his plans and with whom he spends his time. You don't want him to be around other interesting or attractive women; you feel threatened when he is.

Insecurity can cause you to be demanding and have unrealistic expectations of your relationship. When he hurts or disappoints you, you can be upset for days. You live with the fear of doing the wrong thing and losing him. You constantly feel the need to "define" your relationship and talk about your love for each other. You feel that you must show your love for him in greater and greater ways.

Insecurity fills the relationship with frustration and worry. You think, "I can't live with or without him!" You find yourself scheming to keep him.

Lisa even told her boyfriend she was pregnant so he would make a commitment to marry her. Her well-devised plan backfired as she had to go deeper and deeper into the lie when her new husband discovered she was not. She felt she would experience happiness and security only when he was hers. Instead her scheming caused guilt, making her feel alienated from him. His anger toward her for being married before he felt ready resulted in great difficulty in their relationship.

INSECURITY AND A LOVE-TANK DEFICIT

If your father was absent, your love tank needs supernatural filling by your heavenly Father. You can become secure in Jesus as He fills your heart deficit. It is not surprising that many of my daughter's friends did not have fathers present in their lives. Whenever I could, I would encourage these fatherless girls to go home and get a Bible concordance and look for all the verses that talk about God as Father. Fatherless girls can have their love tanks filled as they grasp the reality of God as Father.

And do not call anyone on earth "father," for you have one Father, and He is in heaven (Matthew 23:9 NIV).

Papa God can fill the hole left by a father who abandoned his family. Growing in your understanding of the love of God as Father will help fill your love tank. This is important, because love-tank deficits are readily exploited by the enemy. A loser guy can capitalize on a gal's love hunger, because it often produces a craving for male attention and affection. How critical it is for a daughter to become aware that her absent father—whether absent physically or emotionally—can make her more vulnerable to a ravenous hunger for a boyfriend.

I am not trying to overwhelm you, but to lovingly address what I have seen for years in the lives of girls whose dads were never there for them. In fact, when I hear parents say, "Oh we've had an amicable divorce," I almost start screaming right on the spot. I wrote the book *Free Yourself to Love: the Liberating Power of Forgiveness*, because by God's grace, I've learned how to forgive the unforgivable. In the book I spell *amicable divorce* a little differently from Webster's Dictionary. I spell it *amica-bull divorce*, because it is absolute bull to say anybody is divorced amicably! It's never good.

Amicable is described as lacking in antagonism. Yet ironically, while the antagonism between the spouses may cease with divorce, the ongoing internal antagonism in each child has just begun. The denial concerning the consequences for our children is inestimable!

Love-tank hunger is a very common consequence that enhances a girl's capacity to become Bozo bait. If you are in this situation right now, I want to encourage you: every night before you close your eyes, pray "Oh Jesus, fill my love tank." It is a great prayer to cry out in the car as you drive to work or as you put the dishes in the dishwasher. "Fill my love tank, Lord."

Let me share some proof of this reality in the heart of a ravenously hungry gal. When I was just a young teenager, I already had a huge love-hunger deficit. Although my parents were not divorced, the abuse I experienced from my father produced a Grand Canyon-sized deficit in the love tank of my heart. As a new Christian reading the Bible for the first time, I came across Matthew 23:9 that states, *"Do not call anyone on earth 'father,' for you have one Father, and He is in heaven"* (NIV).

With childlike faith I claimed God as my only true Father. Forty-seven years later, I can still remember declaring, "I claim you Father God as *my* Papa." Still living in an abusive home, I would constantly remind myself of the love of my heavenly Papa.

Praise be to the God and Father of our Lord Jesus Christ, the Father of compassion and the God of all comfort (2 Corinthians 1:3 NIV).

Father God so filled my love tank that I was able to wait for God's best rather than settle for a Bozo. Secure in God, I waited for my Boaz, whom I've now had for thirty-nine years. So my love-tank deficit was compensated by my incomparable Father God.

LOVE-TANK DEFICIT FUELS THIS LIE

Why do women feel they have to go after men? Many women have believed a lie. They think, "I must get the best for myself because God may not give it to me." What do you think would have been the outcome of Ruth's life if she had chosen to believe this lie? Would she have returned home with Orpah and married one of the local guys? Would she have followed Naomi to a new land, but taken control of her own destiny in choosing a mate to care for herself and her mother-in-law? With these poor choices, her life of blessing and joy found in Boaz would not have happened, and we would have missed the blessing of a book such as Ruth.

**Don't settle for less than God's best. Surrender the
terrible burden of always needing life on your terms.**

Ladies, God gives you the choice between His plans and yours. In the midst of her circumstances, Ruth could not have possibly seen that a man like Boaz would one day be her prince. Neither can you with your limited perspective see who or where your prince will be. Only God has all things in view. Are you trying to control your own life? Are you making plans for your life that only God should make? Don't settle for less than God's best. Surrender the terrible burden of always needing life on your terms. Don't look back one day and regret that you made your "life-mate" choice from a limited perspective because you longed for the security of a relationship. God can and will give you His best if you wait for it.

SECURE LOVE

Women tend to struggle with insecurity because of the unique way God created them. God made every little girl with the need to love and be loved by her earthly father. God designed His world with a picture of a family as the theme. The father protects, loves, and cares for his wife and their children. The ideal earthly father models the gentle, nurturing love of the heavenly Father. Many young women in our society did not have a father who followed God's design. This God-given need for a father's love caused a deficit in their lives.

Karen described it this way:

I never really felt loved the way I needed to be. I wanted someone I could love and who would love me in the deepest way. I met and dated a wonderful man. He was a Christian, good-looking, popular, and best of all, he loved me. A deep wonderful friendship with him flourished for almost two years. I wanted to be his wife, but he was not making any move toward a commitment. I was a 21-year-old virgin. I wanted to keep him so badly that I knew I was willing to do anything. I did not intentionally plan to compromise my high standards, but I felt if I were intimate with him, it would show my deep commitment to him, and I would be able to keep him.

As a child I wanted my dad to really love me, but I never seemed to gain his love. I thought this man could fill that need for love that I felt. I was wrong. I lost both my virginity and my closest friend with one act. I believe if I had dealt with the insecurity in my life, I would have seen clearly that no man could meet the heartfelt need for secure love I wanted.

EPIDEMIC OF INSECURITY AMONG WOMEN

"Insecurity among women is epidemic, but it is not incurable. Don't expect it to go away quietly, however. We're going to have to let truth scream louder to our souls than the lies that have infected us,"[1] says Beth Moore, and I agree.

The father of lies (see John 8:44) screams lies at our hearts daily. We can only scream back if our hearts are wallpapered with the truth (see John 8:32). We, as well as our girls, need to learn how to *scream at the liar!* It may seem a contradiction of a Lady in Waiting to be screaming, but there are times when we need to.

When I was a young Christian, I would often have thoughts of worthlessness. I can remember when I first began to exercise appropriate screaming at the enemy of my soul. I was walking to my car after sharing my heart with some teen girls, and as I was backing my car out of the church parking lot I had this thought: "If those girls knew what a loser I really am, they would never listen to me!"

I can still feel how quickly those tears came to my eyes and how swiftly the thoughts of worthlessness poured into my heart. But as quickly as this attack of insecurity invaded my soul, I remembered a verse that I had just learned, Revelation 12:10-11 (NIV):

For the accuser of our brothers, who accuses them before our God day and night, has been hurled down. They overcame him by the blood of the Lamb and by the word of their testimony; they did not love their lives so much as to shrink from death.

As I thought about the 24/7 lying accuser of all Christians, I—as boldly as a teenager could—screamed, "You can go back to where you belong because I belong to Jesus and His blood is my confidence!"

That screaming moment in my car became a confidence framework for the many times in the future when I would face demonized accusations, and would overcome the liar with the scream of truth! Let me share a glimpse of the confidence that allows me to scream back at the assaults of insecurity that plague all women—young and not so young.

WITH GOD, WHO COULD BE AGAINST HER?

Have you ever been criticized so harshly that the pain knocked the breath right out of you? I lived in a household where this was part of the daily schedule! One day a godly woman said to me, "Whenever you are criticized, consider the source, and that will help you monitor your reaction."

I thought a long time about the expression, "consider the source," and I became so excited about this *fact:* God, who knows me through and through, still chose me for Himself.

God's foreknowledge did not keep Him from choosing a sinner like me. Without foreknowledge, people make some serious mistakes, but God, who is all knowing, never makes mistakes and is never caught off guard. This all-knowing God did not choose against me, but for me.

Whenever I am criticized, I first ask the Lord to show me any aspect of the criticism that may be truth, so I can repent and let Jesus transform that blind spot in my life. When the criticism contradicts something that Jesus says about me, I choose to value Jesus' opinion rather than people's opinions. Whatever people say about me, I accept; but I lay the comments alongside Jesus' biographical sketch of me, because that is where I live, rest, and have confidence. Jesus' biographical sketch for one of His girls would read something like this:

- She is chosen and dearly loved by *Me* (see 1 Thess. 1:4; Col. 3:12).

- She is a child of *Mine*, part of *My* family (see Rom. 8:15-16).

- She is free to call God "Daddy" (see Gal. 4:6).

- She was on His mind before He spoke the world into existence (see 2 Tim. 1:9).

- She is one of a kind, custom designed by *God* (see Eph. 2:10).

- She is getting better with every passing moment (see 2 Cor. 5:17).

- She is part of a royal calling and responsibility (see 1 Pet. 2:9-10).

- She is an heir of an unshakable Kingdom (see Gal. 4:6-7; Heb. 12:28).

- She is aware of her enemy, but confident in Papa God (see 1 Pet. 5:8).

The next time someone speaks to you in a harsh and critical manner, just pause and think: *Excuse me; do you know to whom you are speaking?* That thought always puts a smile on my face (and my smile puzzles the one who would slay me verbally).

Why do we continue to allow people's rejection (or imagined rejection) to control us more than the acceptance we have received from God Almighty through Jesus?

In face of all this, what is there left to say? If God is for us, who can be against us? (Romans 8:31 PNT).

As a little girl, you may remember feeling the desire to be cherished, loved, and accepted by your daddy. If he failed to show that love to you in God's way, perhaps you continued to search for a man who would. No man, not even a husband, can fill the need you have for secure love. Only Jesus, who *"is the same yesterday and today and forever,"* will never disappoint or fail you (Heb. 13:8).

Why do we continue to allow people's rejection (or imagined rejection) to control us more than the acceptance we have received from God Almighty through Jesus?

Turn to your heavenly Father now. Pour out to Him your heart's longing to be loved. See His arms open wide and His empty lap ready to embrace and hold you near. He considers you dear. He longs to give you satisfying love. Perhaps He does desire to give you a man to love also. But the man you marry cannot meet your need for security. Only God's love brings security.

MANIPULATION AND MANEUVERING

When you see a woman going after the guys, you probably don't immediately say, "Yes, I see that she really is insecure!" Insecurity dwells in the heart. What you see outwardly is a woman's age-old ability to manipulate and maneuver. When a woman manipulates a situation, she feels personal satisfaction because she believes she is in control.

At one college, a new student arrived who was one of the most attractive guys ever to arrive on campus. In fact, whenever he walked by, the air would move because of all the gasping women. When he walked into the dining hall, the females would suddenly stop talking. (That alone was a miracle!)

Linda, who worked in the Dean of Men's office, had a myriad of females ask for his class schedule. Why would his class schedule be significant? Such information offered a chance for a "life-changing" experience. These silly women would find out his daily schedule and, as soon as their classes ended, would *run* to wherever he would most likely be walking, and "just happen" to be standing on the corner as he passed. Daily, these committed manipulators "just happened" to see him after English literature and then "just happened" to see him after World Civics. Such a schedule definitely kept these gals in peak aerobic condition as daily they frantically tried to arrive in his personal hemisphere.

Beware of the Compulsion for Completion

A number of years ago, I heard the psychologist Dr. Leslie Parrot use a term that perfectly describes how an insecure person is motivated. She coined the term "a compulsion for completion," defined as: If you try to build intimacy with another person before you have done the hard work of becoming whole on your own in Jesus, then all your relationships become an attempt to complete yourself, and it sets you up for failure.

This compulsion for completion is often the fuel behind a gal's manipulative maneuvering. A gal who is confident in the love of God and the love of her family will not struggle with a debilitating compulsion for completion. She will also comprehend that *only God* can complete her—not a man, child, or powerful career.

Resist Being a Surrogate Helpmate

Manipulation and maneuvering can also take the form of serving as a "surrogate helpmate" (suitable helper). Many women want to marry as badly as they want to go to Heaven. They long to care for a man, so they run around trying to find at least a "generic" version of the real thing. These precious (but deceived) women constantly look for a man with a need and pounce on that need in hopes of eventually winning the affection of the man. Any male in need irresistibly attracts them.

For example, a single man at a conference mentioned his need for some name tags, and a mob of women scurried to get tags for him. It was like a race, or a spring sale at the mall! One typical surrogate overheard that a man needed his house cleaned because his parents were coming for a visit. The young man had little time to do it himself because he had been so busy helping at his church, so he made his need known. This "Martha" decided to help the needy man, but didn't check her motive. She assumed that he would appreciate her help so much that he would repay her with some extra attention, perhaps even a date. At the same time, she knew that one of her female friends at the church also had a need, yet Martha would not lift a finger to help her catch up domestically.

What is the difference? Women may find more pleasure doing for a man than a woman because the potential "payoff" seems more valuable. She envisions surrendering her "surrogate" apron for an engagement ring. A wise woman once said, "Do not do for a brother that which you would not do for a sister." Brownies often are baked for the best-looking and most desirable guys, but seldom for the average Joe. (How all these guys stay slim is a miracle—except for their constant running from all the aggressive, manipulative women.)

A "manipulator" may hear of a female friend who needs help and callously allow her to do without it. But if one handsome guy even slightly alludes to his desire for something to drink, she may "crawl across broken glass" to get him a cool drink, all the while quoting Scripture about giving a cup of cool water to him who is thirsty. Allow God to use you to minister to brothers and sisters equally with no ulterior motives. In the beginning, Ruth ministered not to a desirable man, but to a bitter widow—her mother-in-law, at that!

…OR SURROGATE MOM

Another form of maneuvering is to become the guy's "mom." Insecure females all too often deceive themselves into thinking that because they do so much for a particular young man, they will surely win his love. *Wrong!* It is easy for a man, whether he is young or old, to let a woman sacrifice for him. Why? Most men are used to the sacrifices of a woman. Good ol' mom has been sacrificing for him since the womb. Sure, the young man will say, "Thanks," but young men do not marry their mothers! When a woman does something really nice for a certain guy, he usually does not spend the rest of the day thinking about her unselfish service (he may be accustomed to receiving). The woman may begin to feel used.

**When a woman does something really nice for
a certain guy, he usually does not spend the rest of
the day thinking about her unselfish service.**

Some women prepare meals, sew on buttons, and wash the guy's clothes—all the things a mom would do—assuming all this is practice for their future together. Inevitably, the man she has served so unselfishly may fall for a girl who can't bake or sew and thinks you take all clothes to the dry cleaners that "fluff and fold."

Elisabeth Elliot says she is often asked the question, "What can I do to get him to notice me?" Note carefully the advice she gives:

My answer is "nothing." That is, nothing toward the man. Don't call him. Don't write a little note with a smiley face or a flower or fish under the signature and put it in his campus mailbox. Don't slide up to him in the hall and gasp, "I've just got to talk to you!" Don't look woebegone, don't ignore him, don't pursue him, don't do him favors, don't talk about him to nine carefully selected listeners.

There is one thing you can do: turn the whole business over to God. If he's the man God has for you, *"No good thing does He withhold from those who walk uprightly"* (Ps. 84:11). Direct your energies to obedience, not to nailing the man. God has His own methods of getting the two of you together. He doesn't need any help or advice from you.[2]

Notice the word *nothing*. Maybe this little dose of reality will help you constantly check your motives whenever relating to a guy.

MOTIVE CHECK

This is not to say that you cannot do nice things for a man; it is simply a warning to check your motives. A woman with selfish motivation mentally plots the next maneuver to capture the attention of the man of her dreams. Before you go to another activity to spend time with the available guys, as you check your hair and makeup and teeth, give yourself a thorough "heart flossing." Ask the Lord to reveal any impure motive that resides in your heart. Before you bake one more thing for a brother or purchase one more book or meaningful card, be very careful to check your motive and honestly respond to whatever the Lord shows you. You can save yourself many tears and much frustration if you are just willing to do a regular "motive check" on your heart.

To keep your motives pure, check them daily. Proverbs 16:2 (NIV) says, *"All a man's* [woman's] *ways seem innocent to him* [her], *but motives are weighed by the Lord."*

Manipulation and maneuvering can be deadly. If you maneuver to get a man, you will have to maneuver to keep him! This is not implying that there is no work involved in a good relationship, but there is a huge difference between working and maneuvering. You recognize the difference between the two by discerning your motive. Refuse to be a member of the M/M (Manipulation and Maneuvering) Team!

QUITTING THE HUNT

To quit the hunt and stop "going after the guys," you must first avoid maneuvering and manipulating. Ruth did, and God can give you the grace to do it too. Believe that God will take care of you regardless of your circumstances. Don't put your own devices to work. You can only see the outward man from today's perspective. God sees men's hearts from the perspective of eternity.

With His perspective, He can see much better what you need. Trust Him and let Him show you His dependable love for you.

Second, you must put your security in Christ. He longs for you to be secure in His love. He wants to protect, lead, and love you. To develop security, give your heart and emotions to the Lord.

Debby remembers a specific time in her life when she pictured herself before the Lord. In her mind's eye she imagined His loving, kind, Father's face. She pictured herself bringing her broken, lonely heart to her heavenly Father after yet another love bubble had been burst. Debby specifically gave the Lord her love life that day. She prayed:

Father, my heart is fragile and delicate and easily broken. I have tried to find one who will cherish me, without Your view. My heart has been broken and my emotions bruised. I ask You to take and guard my heart. I will choose not to entertain thoughts and emotions of love which cause me to give my heart away too readily. I will come quickly to You when I start feeling like I am in love. Please hold the key to my heart and emotions until a day I can give it to the man You have prepared for me.

Debby has often said what a difficult turning point this was for her. She wanted to trust the Lord with this precious area of her life, but had nagging feelings that she might never again have the giddy, delightful feelings of love. As she dated, she spent time in prayer before and after dates to make sure her heart and emotions were still in the Father's hands. Many times she feared she would never feel those "heart leaps of love," but instead would just marry one of the "nice" guys she had dated.

**I will choose not to entertain thoughts and emotions
of love which cause me to give my heart away too readily. I will
come quickly to You when I start feeling like I am in love.**

One day, as she was praying, she realized she had come to really care for a man named Bill in a special way. They had been dating for several months, and the temptations to let her emotions run wild were very real. Instead, she wrote this in her journal:

> I feel as though I really care for Bill in a deep way. You know what is best for me, Father. I have given my heart to You and my emotions, too. I will wait for a clearer indication that he is my knight in shining armor than just how I feel. You will not allow my heart to be broken again if I leave it with You. I trust You to keep me calm and waiting on Your best timing.

A formula she wrote in her prayer journal to help her keep perspective was this: *With Jesus first and my boyfriend second, I will have lasting peace and security.*

All this may sound like a good idea, but how do you begin? To build security into your life, spend time in God's Word. Proverbs 1:33 says to listen to God and live securely. As you do, you will find out what God is really like—what His character is—not just what you think or have heard He is like. You will be surprised at how differently He sees you than what you have thought.

Read through the Psalms and write down the many promises He has made to you if you are a believer. Psalm 16:11 (KJV) says, *"Thou wilt shew me the path of life* [married or not]; *in Thy presence is fulness of joy* [His presence, not marriage, brings joy]; *at Thy right hand there are pleasures for evermore."* (What more could a girl ask for?)

By spending time in God's Word, you will also learn what God thinks of you. In First Peter 2:4, God says you are choice and precious to Him. He calls you precious, honored, loved, and His redeemed one in Isaiah 43:1-6. Isaiah 43:7 says you were created for His glory. You are very special to God—so special that He has plans for you: *"plans for* [your] *welfare and not for calamity to give you a future and a hope"* (Jer. 29:11).

The New Testament is also full of God's thoughts of you. You are accepted (see Rom. 15:7); you are not condemned (see Rom. 8:1); and you are His child (see John 1:12). (By the way, the female child of a King is a *princess.* Act like the valuable princess you are, and plan to be treated as royalty.) You also are the temple of God (see 1 Cor. 3:17). He is your adequacy (see 2 Cor. 3:5), and He leads you in His triumph (see 2 Cor. 2:14). His love letter to you, the Bible, is full of all the wonderful things He says about you.

Do not allow insecurity to motivate you to maneuver or manipulate your relationships. Instead of hunting for a husband or boyfriend, concentrate on becoming a woman of excellence (see Ruth 3:11). As a Lady of Security, wait for your heavenly Father to bring about His perfect plans for you.

ELEVEN TRUTHS TO STRENGTHEN SECURITY AND DEFUSE INSECURITY

We…are being transformed into the same image from glory to glory, just as from the Lord, the Spirit (2 Corinthians 3:18).

Truth #1— Do Not Label Yourself Negatively

• Self-condemnation leaves no room for loving others.

• If you're hard on yourself, you're hard on others.

…Love your neighbor as yourself (Matthew 22:39).

Truth #2—Behave Assertively, With God-Confidence

• God-confidence is the opposite of arrogance and pride.

For God did not give us a spirit of timidity, but a spirit of power, of love and of self-discipline (2 Timothy 1:7 NIV).

Truth #3—When You Fail, Confess and Refuse to Condemn Yourself

• If you fail, it only means you still have a pulse.

*If we confess our sins, he is faithful and just and **will forgive** us our sins…* (1 John 1:9 NIV).

There is now no condemnation for those who are in Christ Jesus (Romans 8:1 NIV).

Truth #4—Do Not Compare Yourself with Others

- Comparisons are demoralizing.

- You are unique, one of a kind; therefore you are incomparable.

...When they measure themselves by themselves and compare themselves with themselves, they are not wise (2 Corinthians 10:12 NIV).

Truth #5—Concentrate on God's Grace

- A definition of grace: for one to bow down in order to benefit another/others greatly.

- Grace is strength allotted to me to behave myself.

How great is the love the Father has lavished on us, that we should be called children of God! And that is what we are! (1 John 3:1 NIV).

Truth #6—Associate with Positive People

- As we associate, we become.

- Your closest friend is a mirror of the future you!

He who walks with the wise grows wise... (Proverbs 13:20 NIV).

Truth #7—Learn How to Rejoice in All Things

- The key facet of emotional health is the ability to be thankful and grateful.

Give thanks in all circumstances, for this is God's will for you in Christ Jesus (1 Thessalonians 5:18 NIV).

Truth #8—Have Realistic Expectations of Yourself and Others

- Remember, on your best day...you are still "but dust" (see Ps. 103:13-14).

- The source of so much grief: unrealistic expectations (see Ps. 39:7).

...Do not think of yourself more highly than you ought, but rather think of yourself with sober judgment... (Romans 12:3 NIV).

Truth #9—Growth and Change Are a Process and Are Never Instantaneous

- God is the Agent of Change (see John 17:17).

- The start is the promise of the finish (see Phil. 1:6; 1 Thess. 5:24).

- In God's corrections, He never stops believing in us!

For whom the Lord loves He reproves, even as a father, the son in whom he delights (Proverbs 3:12).

Truth #10—Do What Is Right and Pleasing to Jesus

- Pleasing Jesus is not the same as pleasing people (see Matt. 6:1).

- How do you discern the difference between people pleasing and "Papa pleasing?" (See Hebrews 4:12-13.)

If I were still trying to please men, I would not be a servant of Christ (Galatians 1:10 NIV).

Truth #11—Be Positive

- Consider fasting from critical remarks.

- See how long you can go without saying something negative.

- Pray for a mouth filter:

Finally, brothers, whatever is true, whatever is noble, whatever is right, whatever is pure, whatever is lovely, whatever is admirable—if anything is excellent or praiseworthy—think about such things (Philippians 4:8 NIV).

Learning to sit still,
Resting in His will,
Confident to abide,
With Him by my side,
Resisting manipulation,
Waiting only for His stipulations. —*JMK*

BECOMING A LADY OF SECURITY

- Look at the things most important to you, the things on which you spend the most of your time and energy (e.g., appearance, money, career, family, friendships, dates). If these were taken away, how would you be affected? Security is basing one's life on what cannot be taken away. Are you building your life on what makes you secure or insecure?

- Do you find yourself manipulating for friendships with guys? Proverbs 4:23 exhorts you to watch over your heart. Write out ways you can respond when the temptation to "scheme" for a date comes your way.

- Meditate on Colossians 3:1-3. How could these verses help you the next time you feel insecure and want to take future matters into your own hands?

- Discuss the quote: "Compulsion for Completion: If you try to build intimacy with another person before you have done the hard work of becoming whole on your own in Jesus, then all your relationships become an attempt to complete yourself, and it sets you up for failure."

- What can a Lady in Waiting do with her feelings while she waits? List them from Psalm 37:3-7.

- In your journal confess any times you sought to manipulate a person or situation. Seek to put your security in your King and ask His Holy Spirit for help.

- How would having your security in the Lord and not in whom you are dating affect you if the dating relationship ended? Could you be grateful for a friendship even without the promise of a future? Being secure in God's forever love (see Heb. 13:5) allows a woman to build relationships for friendship, not merely romance for a future.

- Eleven Truths to Strengthen Security and Defuse Insecurity: consider working through each of these principles in your daily quiet time!

ENDNOTES

1. Beth Moore, *So Long Insecurity: You've Been a Bad Friend to Us* (Carol Stream, IL: Tyndale House Publishers, 2010), xiii.

2. Elisabeth Elliot, *Passion and Purity* (Old Tappan, NJ: Fleming H. Revell Company, 1984), 59–60.

Chapter 8

LADY OF CONTENTMENT

You have just returned home from a great singles' retreat where you once again surrendered your frustrations as a single in exchange for God's peace and contentment. As you listen to your answering machine, you hear a certain voice. The most sought-after bachelor you know asks you for a date next weekend. Do you remain calm and give your expectations to the Lord? Or do you jump back in your car and head to the mall to register your china and look at some wedding gowns? Would the prospect of a date with the most eligible bachelor in town cause you to experience the "Pre-romantic Stress Disorder"? Or would you surrender your expectations to Jesus?

For a single woman to experience genuine contentment while soloing in a "couples' world," she must avoid the ditches of discontentment. She needs to learn the mystery of contentment and its power over the restless torture of desire.

THE TORTURE OF DESIRE

It has been said that suffering is having what you do not want (singleness), and wanting what you do not have (a husband). As a single woman, you would probably scream "Amen" to such a description of suffering. You know what it is like to get up each day knowing that you do not have what you want—a husband. How do you cope with such a longing?

Longing for what you do not have is a universal condition. It is not limited to singles. It is true that the longing for a husband can be satisfied on your wedding day, but that longing is soon replaced by desires and expectations about the marriage relationship that may not be satisfied in a thousand lifetimes. If you are presently discontent as a single woman, you can count on being dissatisfied as a married woman in the future.

The mystery of contentment often seems to escape the understanding of the single woman. She assumes that her circumstances justify her condition and give her permission to remain dissatisfied with her life assignment. Not having learned how to lay down the terrible burden of always wanting life to be on her terms, she continues to struggle with the torture of her desires. The restlessness caused by her desire for what she does not have makes waiting seem an impossible task. In fact, to the discontented woman, the word *wait* probably compares to a cuss word in her mind. A Lady in Waiting finds her capacity to wait for God's best to be rooted in contentment.

Counseling married women for more than three decades, I can assure you that singles are not the most discontent gals I know. I know more discontent married women than single women. Singles really believe deep in their souls that their discontentment would end if they just had their Mr. Right. Ironically, I know plenty of women who got their Mr. Right, *but they are discontent about so much in their marriage that doesn't match their expectations and dreams.*

CONTENTMENT AND UNREALISTIC EXPECTATIONS

In the letter to the Philippians, Paul writes from prison about a godly contentment that he, himself, had to learn. I believe we can strengthen our understanding of the mystery of contentment by looking at *unrealistic expectations* that assault our contentment daily.

One day my son shared a quote with me that described this condition precisely. The quote so captured my heart that I modified it and wrote it on a slip of paper and taped it to the dashboard of my car: "Expectations are premeditated resentment."[1]

Throughout that day, as I drove around doing errands, I replayed hundreds of situations from my life where I could clearly trace the expectations that preceded the resentment in my heart. Then I remembered a quote characterizing resentment as "drinking poison and hoping the other person dies."

If my expectations are inextricably linked to premeditated resentment, then I am poisoning myself—unless I immediately commit those expectations to God (see Ps. 62:5). I kept thinking of the holidays, parties, and many social gatherings when my expectations of certain people were so high that it would inevitably spoil the occasion for me. I can't even begin to number the holidays I ruined through my unrealistic expectations of family and friends!

If my expectations are inextricably linked to premeditated resentment, then I am poisoning myself— unless I immediately commit those expectations to God.

Want a "Ten" but Keep Getting a "Five"?

Here is a story about one of those many discontented women I mentioned and what she learned. She is a dear friend of mine who had been battling depression that was fueled by a deep discontentment. If you looked at this woman's life, you would start screaming, *"How can you possibly be depressed or discontent?"* She had it *all;* but having it all had not kept her from constantly struggling with a low-grade fever that ran through her soul.

Finally, she had an epiphany in the counselor's office when she was introduced to the principle of wanting a "ten" life in a "five" world. The counselor helped her to see that she wanted something (a *ten* life) that doesn't exist outside the Garden of Eden, where *five* is too often the realistic number. The woman's absurd expectations were fueling her constant trouble with depression.

In various ways, we are all like this woman; we want life to be a ten. We wanted to be married by twenty-seven—or at least thirty—then have children at just the right time in our biological schedule or career path. Then we wanted to go to family gatherings without any conflict, especially during the holidays. We wanted to be able to have it all—hubby, kids, house, career, great friends, perfect vacation—the list goes on and on. All these expectations set us up for inevitable disappointment, discontentment and offense—multiple layers of these struggles.

Now we are ready for the Five vs. Ten Theory. When we learn to expect offenses, we are prepared for days or events that are more fives than tens. If you prepare to go to an event, especially one where you were previously offended or disappointed, and you accept its potential as a five, but it turns out to be an eight, then you end up feeling like you've received a bonus.

Recently I went on a dream trip to Hawaii with my husband. The whole time I was packing I was praying about my dreamy expectations. I kept giving the trip to God, and consequently, when I got very sick on the trip, I didn't go into a whining temper tantrum, *because I had already yielded my expectations to God.* I didn't have to drag myself from whining to worship. I did not go to Hawaii expecting a ten so when I got a six, I didn't return home in deep depression and discontentment. Every dream not yielded to God is a nightmare getting ready to happen (see Ps. 39:7 and 62:5).

THE CAPACITY TO WAIT

Circumstantially, Ruth had the perfect excuse to be discontented. Widowed at a young age, her circumstances provided the perfect breeding ground for self-pity and bitterness. In fact, her mother-in-law changed her own name from *Naomi* (pleasant) to *Mara* (bitter) to signify her discontentment. Yet Ruth chose to cling to the God of Israel, whom she found to be trustworthy, even in difficult circumstances.

Contentedly facing each day's task, Ruth received the attention and blessing of the most eligible bachelor in town. Then Naomi told her that Boaz was a candidate for being their kinsman-redeemer (see the Levirate Law in

Deuteronomy 25:5-10). This simply meant that the Mosaic Law allowed Boaz, as the closest kin, to redeem the childless widow and keep the family name alive. The law could even require that Boaz marry Ruth. Can you imagine finding the most eligible bachelor and saying to him, "The law requires you to marry me before my thirtieth birthday"?

Naomi instructs Ruth to approach Boaz and ask him if he would be their kinsman-redeemer. This episode is covered in chapter 3 of the Book of Ruth. Boaz's response to Ruth's request is precious: *"And now, my daughter, don't be afraid. I will do for you all you ask. All my fellow townsmen know that you are a woman of noble character"* (Ruth 3:11 NIV). Can you imagine any man saying to you, "I will do for you all you ask"? His willingness was directly related to the character he had noticed in her responses to life and God.

Ruth returns home with the good news. Naomi, however, does not immediately respond by taking her daughter-in-law to the mall to look for a wedding gown. An anxious and discontented woman would think that a willing and interested bachelor is enough motivation for ordering wedding invitations. But for the Lady of Contentment, this would be inappropriate behavior.

Naomi's response to Boaz's willingness may have put a damper on most single women's racing heartbeat: *"Then Naomi said, 'Wait, my daughter, until you find out what happens. For the man will not rest until the matter is settled today'"* (Ruth 3:18 NIV). Who has to *wait?* The woman must wait. Who is the one who will not rest? The man, Boaz, will not rest.

WAIT

Such an assignment is not to cause suffering, but to prevent it. Women experience so much needless pain when they run ahead of God's format. Naomi knew that there may exist an even closer kinsman who would qualify to redeem her and Ruth. (In fact, there was a kinsman closer than Boaz whom she did not know about, but he would be disqualified by a former pledge.) Naomi did not want Ruth's heart to race ahead into disappointment in case the circumstances did not go as assumed.

DISCONTENTMENT SUFFOCATES JOY

When we find ourselves discontented, we are all too often focusing on what is missing from our lives rather than seeing what is going well with them. Ruth could have focused entirely on being a young widow. She could have walked about Bethlehem in a constant, self-focused mourning state. But this is not the picture we are given in Scripture. Ruth trusted God with her circumstances and went about working in the barley harvest rather than focusing on "poor me."

Too many gals think they are joyless because they are boyfriend-less. The irony is that they are joyless because they are not content with God's will for their lives.

Comparing one's life circumstances with others' is always suffocating. Discontentment is fed by unfair comparisons. When you compare anything about yourself with someone else—even if that someone is your BFF—comparison will inevitably suffocate your joy. Paul the apostle warned us about this discontentment that flows from foolish comparisons.

For who makes you different from anyone else? What do you have that you did not receive? And if you did receive it, why do you boast as though you did not? (1 Corinthians 4:7 NIV)

The archenemy of contentment is self-pity. For many years I viewed self-pity as emotional weakness. Then a godly man corrected my perception. I learned that self-pity is just inverted pride, and pride is never weakness. When people feel discontent and sorry for themselves, they are quite likely angry because they didn't get what they wanted. Pride feeds an overinflated view of what one deserves.

The archenemy of contentment is self-pity.

"Self-pity is easily the most destructive of non-pharmaceutical narcotics; it is addictive, gives momentary pleasure and separates the victim from reality."[2]

Ask Jesus to help you not allow the emotional vampires of discontentment and self-pity to drain you of your joy in the Lord.

DITCHES OF DISCONTENTMENT

Being single can be difficult enough for a woman, but the heartbreak from being "led on" by a man can dangerously lead to a ditch of discontentment. Some women are so emotionally scarred from falling into such a ditch that it literally takes them years to recover and rediscover the capacity to trust any male in their lives.

Why some males are unaware of their capacity to defraud is still a mystery. *"And that no man transgress and defraud his brother* [sister] *in the matter because the Lord is the avenger in all these things..."* (1 Thess. 4:6). To defraud is to excite physical or emotional desires that cannot be righteously fulfilled. Since many men do not realize how their actions defraud their sisters in Christ, single women need to be aware of common situations where a guy might lead a woman on. When aware of such techniques, a single woman can avoid unnecessary heartbreak and more effectively keep a rein on her emotions.

One way a guy may lead a woman on is by the unwise things he may say or do. A wonderful single guy started a letter one day with the words *Dear Sunshine*. When asked who this "Dear Sunshine" was, he said it was his nickname for a girl at college. He came up with this affectionate nickname for her one evening while they stood on a hill overlooking the school as the sun was setting. When asked if they were dating, he replied, "Oh, no, we're just friends, and there isn't any future for our relationship." He was encouraged to stop calling her Sunshine because it would defraud her emotionally. But, like many men, he had a hard time understanding that calling her Sunshine might cause her to dream about being the "sunshine" in his future after they graduate.

A second way a man might defraud a woman is by ascribing to an unwritten code that has been distributed by Hollywood and swallowed by most of Christianity: friendships with the opposite sex must be romantic and must not establish any emotional boundaries. What Hollywood advocates is like body surfing on the crest of an emotional wave. To establish boundaries seems like an attack on love. Ironically, limits *protect* real love and leave no room for painful defrauding.

Ken and Jackie established some specific guidelines for their dating relationship in the areas of leadership, communication, and purity. Classmates (even Christians) thought their goals and guidelines would prevent their friendship from blossoming and surviving. Contrary to popular opinion, they have been building on those guidelines for the past thirty-nine years—and romance thrives in their relationship.

In a McDonald's commercial, a guy presented clear guidelines for him and his date. Just before the couple gets to the car, the guy makes one last remark, "I want you to realize that this is just a date, not a commitment, and not a proposal." The girl just smiles and continues toward the car, en route to McDonald's and a movie. Now you may feel his style is just too honest, but such clear communication prevents much misunderstanding between a man's actions and a woman's interpretation of his behavior.

Another way a guy may defraud a woman is by emphasizing the future potential of the relationship rather than focusing on the present opportunities for the friendship to grow. This way of defrauding incites feelings in a woman that cannot be properly fulfilled at that time. This creates emotional turmoil for many women, making it difficult to wait with contentment. Postpone talk of a future together, marriage, or what kind of home you want until engagement. Do not encourage talk of things that "might be"; but rather encourage words and actions that develop the present friendship.

THE ELEVENTH COMMANDMENT

Keeping in mind these common ways that women can be defrauded by men, realize that a single woman can sabotage her own contentment by defrauding herself. A single woman can defraud herself as effectively as can her male counterpart. Protect your contentment by adopting this Eleventh Commandment: Thou shalt not defraud thyself.

**A single woman can sabotage her own
contentment by defrauding herself.**

Women defraud themselves by confusing ministry with matrimony. A guy tries to help a girl grow spiritually, and she sees his care and interest as leading inevitably to marriage. Another guy and girl work on a ministry team together and their spiritual intimacy is confused in her mind with romantic intentions.

Misread intentions between males and females put them on a collision course. The crash can be avoided if the Lady of Contentment would keep in mind that her emotions must be submitted to the facts: ministering together is a privilege as a believer, not an automatic marriage opportunity. Daily, throughout the world, women's hearts are broken because they allow their emotions to run ahead of commitments. Women, young and old, seem to resist controlling their emotions. As a result, they end up emotional cripples, angry at the men who failed to live up to their emotional fantasies.

A most innocent gesture can produce the most elaborate fantasy. A man sends a single woman a thank you card for her vital help in some project or ministry. What is her response to this kind gesture? She laminates the card, anticipates a future with him, and allows her expectations to run rampant.

Counselors are constantly helping men and women properly interpret their relationships. Nancy had been in counseling for more than a year because her heart had been broken and her emotions devastated through defrauding. She told her counselor how she had deceived herself in her relationships with men.

As a new Christian, Nancy joined a large singles ministry where she became very attentive to the various needs of the singles director. She did all the special things that a "mom" often does for her son, or a woman does for her boyfriend. Not only did she attend to his practical needs, but she also was an inspiration to him as she grew by leaps and bounds in the Lord. She unselfishly gave him every spare moment she had, helping him with the many needs he had as the leader of such a huge singles group. If he needed someone to counsel a woman, he always called on her. If a speaker needed a ride to the airport, he called on her. She was a 24-hour crisis line at his disposal. To the undiscerning eye, it all seemed innocent—a very dedicated new Christian enthusiastically serving her singles director. But the lack of discretion on the part of the minister, coupled with her own spiritual immaturity, made a deadly combination. She confused ministry with matrimony and defrauded herself.

After a Christmas trip together where they shared many deep emotions, she went to Israel for a month. When she returned, he greeted her with the shocking news that he had become engaged while she was away. Did he ask the woman who had worked faithfully by his side to share his life and ministry? No. He proposed to a sweet, but less-involved member of the singles group. Needless to say, this devastated Nancy. This is not an isolated incident. The number of single women defrauding themselves seems to have grown to epidemic proportions.

To heed the Eleventh Commandment, you must consciously resist doing another good deed for a man in your life until you know the motive behind your "unselfish" gesture. How many gifts have you already given to some guy in your life because you sensed that the relationship had future dating potential? How many ministries have you participated in because of the chance to be seen by him? How many times have you volunteered to help a brother when you knew you would not be so willing to help a sister in Christ?

The easiest way to break the Eleventh Commandment is to play the "surrogate wife or mother" in relation to a brother in Christ. Some single women pick a worthy recipient of their time and attention, then they tend to any special needs they find out about in the guise of unselfish giving. There are single women who wash the guy's clothes and clean his apartment, but haven't even been on their first date with him. They might as well wash his car also. What these single women do not know is that doing good deeds for a man does not win his love. Why? Most of the time, he is used to a woman waiting on him. Remember good ol' mom?

A dedicated Christian should do good deeds, but when you limit your service to the men in your group, it will ultimately backfire. You can end up feeling bruised by your own self-defrauding when you realize the man has taken your special gestures of service for granted.

One summer, as a member of a traveling drama team, a single woman gave herself unselfishly to a particular guy in the group. For ten weeks, during every free minute, she helped him study to pass his ordination exam, which required pages of memorization. At first, all the help she gave him really impressed the other team members. But as time went on, it became obvious to everyone, except him, that her feelings for him had changed from sisterly love to romantic affection. Was anyone to blame for the pain that came at the end of the summer? If both had more discernment, maybe they could have acted more wisely in their friendship so she would not have been defrauded.

When the tour was over and everyone went their own way, he gave her a hearty hug and big "thank you"—and off he went to his ordination, which was followed by his marriage to a girl from back home. What happened to the one left behind with the big "thank you"? She learned a hard lesson, but she was emotionally devastated. She carelessly allowed herself to give her heart away. She gave hours to someone in the hope of reciprocation, but she ended up empty-handed with only a painful memory of giving so much and getting so little. Her motive was wrong. She defrauded herself through unchecked emotions.

PRENUPTIAL FANTASIES

An important method of limiting your own self-defrauding is through daily discipline over "prenuptial fantasies." Such fantasies may provide you an escape from monotonous reality, but these moments are dangerous. They will aggravate your struggle for contentment because they are not innocent daydreams, but an attack on your godly contentment. You may be so used to daily fantasies that you might not even realize when you begin daydreaming again about your prince.

**A single woman's struggle with contentment
can be traced back to her fantasies more than
to her frustrating circumstances.**

Often a single woman's struggle with contentment can be traced back to her fantasies more than to her frustrating circumstances. Just think for a moment about three words from Second Corinthians 10:5 (KJV): *"Casting down imaginations."* Fantasizing about a future with a guy you have been watching in Sunday school or at work is nothing more than your very active imagination. What should you do when you start daydreaming about a guy you've never dated or even formally met? You must take your thoughts to Jesus and leave them in His capable hands.

This daily discipline of taking your fantasies to Jesus is the foundation for your future as a contented woman, whether you are married or single. Right now they are just prenuptial fantasies, but when you are married, those fantasies about other men could continue.

Lack of discipline in the area of "casting down imaginations" may result in self-defrauding and needless discontentment. Sally did not develop this discipline and was hurt needlessly.

She went as a counselor to a national youth convention and met a sharp Christian guy from her home state. They enjoyed chatting between seminars, and after she returned home, he began calling her long distance. After each phone call, she would dream and talk to her friends about their potential together. She thought about his being younger, but refused to let her fantasy be spoiled by something as insignificant as age. She allowed the fantasy to move into vivid living color after every long-distance phone call. Then her dreams turned into a nightmare. During one of their delightful conversations, he asked her a favor. "Would you mind if I come and visit you during spring break?" That sounded exciting to her, but then he asked the second part of his favor. "Would you mind if I bring two friends?" She assumed he meant two guys he had been discipling, but to her surprise their names were not Bill and John but Sarah and Becky.

After she picked herself up off the floor, she very politely told him that such a plan would not work. When she hung up the phone, she felt angry and betrayed that he apparently wanted to use her home (three blocks from the beach) as a vacation spot. Maybe the guy was insensitive to her, but her hurt was multiplied because she had chosen to spend the preceding days and nights daydreaming about their potential relationship. Her pain and anger could have been reduced if she had exercised some discipline in relation to prenuptial fantasizing about this guy.

Friends too often participate in the development of one's prenuptial fantasies. After only one date with a wonderful man, a girl will share the details of the evening, and her friends will not only share her joy, but also foster excessive imaginings by asking questions like, "Do you think this is the one? Could this be the Boaz you have been waiting so long for?" We not only need the discipline of monitoring our own fantasies, but we also need friends who will remind us not to run ahead of God's timing. Such monitoring of our emotions and accountability between friends is so helpful for the Christian single woman.

SPIRITUAL MONITOR

When a friend excitedly calls to tell you about the evening she has just spent with a special man, you often know before she gets two paragraphs into the telling of the evening where she is going—fantasy land. As she begins to tell you that he is a friend from her past who recently became a Christian and is suddenly back in her life, be careful. As she rattles on at 100 miles an hour, it would be easy to say, "Maybe your Boaz is finally here"—but don't. Remember wise Naomi and avoid defrauding your friend. By enthusiastically building false hope in a situation that could be here today but gone before her next paycheck, you can easily help a friend to defraud herself.

To help her monitor her reactions, point out that one long-distance phone call from a male friend is not reason enough to take him home to meet her parents. Encourage your friend, instead, to wait until she sees how the friendship develops. Your monitoring may not be appreciated at first, but the fruit of such counsel will be sweet. This is not to suggest that you cannot share a friend's joy about a wonderful date with a godly man. But a gift greater than simply sharing her joy is to encourage your friend not to run ahead of the relationship through prenuptial fantasies. Many tears have been shed over relationships that never materialized except in one's dreams.

At a girls' night out, a single woman shared how she used to resent spiritual monitoring from her mom in relation to her fantasies. She used to dread her mother's calm and reserved response to her dramatic presentation of the date she had with the man of her dreams. Her mom, a vivacious woman, seemed so restrained and even a little cynical when responding to her daughter's "bubbly babbling" about Mr. Right. How could such an outgoing, positive, and uplifting mom be so reserved when responding to the dreamy-eyed chatter about the arrival of the man worth waiting for? Did her mom have information of which the daughter was unaware? Had she hired a detective to follow the man of her daughter's dreams and find incriminating information? Of course not! This mom, like Naomi, was extremely wise in monitoring her own response so her daughter would not get excited and distracted by a prospect who might never become a reality.

How refreshing to hear about a wise mom who helped her daughter not to deceive (defraud) herself. Too often moms innocently focus on the famine their daughters face in relation to dating. Instead of encouraging her daughter to use her free time for Jesus (to be a Lady of Diligence), mom and daughter analyze and re-analyze her dateless state and head for the mall to soothe the emptiness. Not everyone has been blessed with a "spiritual monitor" in a mother, but we can learn from this one's example, and we can be spiritual monitors to the single women in our lives.

A spiritual monitor knows the importance of surrendering her own expectations to the only One who can be trusted with her desires and dreams.

How can you begin to be a spiritual monitor? The next time a friend is bubbling over with joy after a date with a wonderful guy, pray for your capacity to share her joy; then pray for the courage to speak the truth about surrendering her dreams to the Lord and not running ahead of Him in her expectations. The spiritual monitor knows the importance of surrendering her own expectations to the only One who can be trusted with her desires and dreams. She can encourage others to surrender their own prenuptial fantasies in exchange for the truth in Psalm 62:5 (KJV): *"My soul, wait thou only upon God; for my expectation is from Him."*

Did you expect to be married by now? Or did you expect to be married forever, and now you are divorced? These expectations mean that you need God's tender loving care and the encouragement of a spiritual monitor who will regularly remind you not to run ahead of the Lord in your relationships with men.

Two women took the challenge to be spiritual monitors to their dearest friend, who was dating Mr. Wonderful. These friends had to consistently resist fanning the fire of their friend's enthusiasm. They monitored their responses and limited their reactions to what was reality and not hopeful fantasy. Because this single woman had waited quite a long time for her Boaz, it would have been easy for her to run with the simplest amount of attention received. But since her best friends monitored their lips, she was free to respond properly to her boyfriend. Unmonitored chatting can lead to major defrauding.

Ironically, the same close friends who help to accelerate the prenuptial fantasy may be the ones who must comfort the lone lovebird when Mr. Right asks another girl out and no more history is to be made with him. Her disappointment will be in direct proportion to the degree that she and her friends responded prematurely to a relationship that will last only in her memory. The next time a friend shares the details of an exciting evening with such a hunk of a guy, don't overreact. Instead, say to her, "I am thrilled that you had a great time. I am so glad you shared your excitement with me. Now do yourself a favor and before you close your eyes to dream tonight, prayerfully commit Mr. Wonderful to Jesus." You will be a true friend and a spiritual monitor for her.

Thousands of needless tears,
Produced by careless cheers,
Assuming that Boaz is finally here,
When the arrival of her prince is not even near…. —JMK

If you do not have a spiritual monitor in a close friend, then ask the Lord to help you find such a friend.

THE MYSTERY OF CONTENTMENT

Whether married or single, in prison or shopping at the mall, the key to enjoying this moment rests with your inner contentment. When your happiness in life is based on "your terms," it is a terrible limitation that will result in a hollow gladness. Singleness does not produce lack of contentment any more than marriage provides contentment. Lack of contentment is the result of the terrible burden of wanting life on your terms.

Married women complain about their lack of contentment as often as single women do, if not more. Both groups of women need to develop the quality of contentment. Paul the apostle, while living in a dark, damp dungeon, wrote of the mystery of contentment that does not depend on circumstances. He described the secret as a "learning process" to which he willingly submitted rather than resisting the conditions:

> *Not that I speak from want, for **I have learned to be content in whatever circumstances I am**. I know how to get along with humble means, and I also know how to live in prosperity; in any and every circumstance I have learned the secret of being filled and going hungry, both of having abundance and suffering need. **I can do all things through Him who strengthens me*** (Philippians 4:11-13).

Whether married or single, one must learn that it is Jesus who strengthens you to walk in the most dismal or delightful of circumstances. True contentment is learned. You are not born with it, and you cannot buy it at one of Kmart's blue-light specials. Your classroom for learning is your daily life. Every shattered dream or unfulfilled expectation serves as a perfect opportunity to learn contentment. These circumstances are your classroom assignments for learning the mystery of contentment.

Learning contentment requires complete dependence upon Jesus, for difficult circumstances without the strength of Jesus can rob you of potential contentment. Do not be deceived into thinking you do not need Jesus' strength to face the good circumstances as well as the bad. When the sun is shining with no clouds in sight, you may assume that you can securely bask in the sunshine without any prospect of rain; however, this full feeling can easily breed a tendency to ignore Jesus: *"Otherwise, I may have too much and disown You and say, 'Who is the Lord?'"* (Prov. 30:9 NIV).

DISCONTENTMENT AND LONELINESS

The schooling in contentment may require us to pay attention to what we run to in our disappointment. Learning to be content when one is "alone" is a developed skill as well. Some people develop this skill at a younger age because of their circumstances or their personalities. For others, it takes genuine training. Being alone without being lonely means that we must grasp that at *this* moment God is fully aware of what is going on in our lives; and *this* moment is in the frame of His plan for us.

Lord, You have assigned me my portion and my cup; You have made my lot secure (Psalm 16:5 NIV).

A dateless Friday night is not a mistake by a loving God. Discontentment, however, flows by focusing on someone else's portion, *her* date with Mr. Wonderful, and my Friday night with the family again!

Being alone without being lonely means that we must grasp that at this moment God is fully aware of what is going on in our lives; and this moment is in the frame of His plan for us.

I agree with Lloyd Ogilvie who wrote, "One of the most crucial discoveries I have made over the years, working with and listening to people, is that loneliness has little to do with the absence of people. We can feel lonely in a crowd, among friends, in a marriage, in the family, at a sorority or fraternity house, and in a church."[3]

Our loneliness cannot always be fixed, but it can always be accepted as the very will of God *for now;* and acceptance turns it into something beautiful. I witnessed this reality up close and personal observing our daughter spending many Friday nights "alone" but not lonely. She learned the discipline of trusting God with lonely moments. When she was excluded from activities because her friends knew her firm standards, Jessi had the tutorial of trusting God with datelessness as well as exclusion.

And remember! God *never* forsakes us. He *never* excludes us. So just like I learned in college, a dateless Friday night is always an opportunity for a date with Jesus!

STOP ARGUING WITH THE UMPIRE

Do you now see the incompatibility of anxiety-filled singleness and contented godliness? Are you ready to rid yourself of the ditches of discontentment that have robbed you of so much peace and joy?

Defrauding by a man, a friend, or even oneself will aggravate your lack of contentment; however, the source of your lack is not defrauding or even frustrating circumstances. Your lack of contentment is because of *pride*. Pride can be described as an excessively high opinion of what one deserves. When a single's life is not moving in the direction she wants (husband, career, children, house, etc.) the arguing often begins. With whom is the single woman arguing? It is none other than the Umpire, the Arbitrator: Jesus. *"Let the peace of Christ rule* [arbitrate, umpire] *in your hearts..."* (Col. 3:15).

The struggle with the Umpire is not limited to the single women up to bat! Every woman who has descended from Eve must learn to trust the call of her heavenly Umpire. The trouble from the beginning was a woman not listening to the Umpire, but reaching out for a life on "her terms." Why would a woman argue with such an all-wise Umpire? *"Pride only breeds quarrels"* (Prov. 13:10 NIV).

Consider a very poignant verse that brilliantly reveals the war in all of us: *"What causes fights and quarrels among you? Don't they come from your desires that battle within you? You want something but don't get it"* (James 4:1-2 NIV). Honestly face any struggle you may have with your pride-driven desire to have life on your terms. Exchange your pride for Jesus' strength so you may accept whatever assignment the Umpire has for you from this moment forward. Dating is not a reward or a prize for living for Jesus. A Friday night without a date is often a night of "being spared" by an all-wise Umpire.

My soul finds rest in God alone (Psalm 62:1 NIV).

RUTH, THE PROVERBS 31 WOMAN, AND CONTENTMENT

The Book of Ruth is a wonderful profile of a young woman learning contentment in a situation that would naturally produce whining. Because Ruth trusted in the God of Israel, she learned how to be content. Learning to be content produced in her life the very qualities extolled in Proverbs 31.

One can't help but wonder whether the writer of Proverbs 31 was inspired by Ruth's awesome example. Oral tradition would have passed the inspiring story of Ruth from generation to generation. With Ruth being the great, great grandmother of King David, it is not a stretch to consider the impact of her story on the writer of Proverbs 31. Consider the following parallels between the woman it describes and Ruth:

- Devoted to her family (see Ruth 1:15-18; Prov. 31:10-12,23)

- Delighted in her work (see Ruth 2:2; Prov. 31:13)

- Diligent in her labor (see Ruth 2:7,17,23; Prov. 31:14-22,24,27)

- Dedicated to godly speech (see Ruth 2:10,13; Prov. 31:26)

- Dependent on God (see Ruth 2:12; Prov. 31:30)

- Dressed with care (see Ruth 3:3; Prov. 31:22,25)

- Discreet with men (see Ruth 3:6-13; Prov. 31:11-12,23)

- Delivered blessings (Ruth 4:14-15; Prov. 31:28,29,31)

When I consider how profoundly the Book of Ruth and Proverbs 31 have impacted me as a woman, I have to ask, "Wouldn't this material be a great little Bible study for any single gal?" Looking up these verses and examining the character qualities that enhanced Ruth's contentment cannot help but strengthen the heart of the Lady of Contentment.

FANTASY HEART GUARD

Okay ladies, it's time to say the Single Woman's Pledge of Allegiance. Place your hand over your heart and repeat after me:

By God's grace I will guard my heart daily.
I will endeavor to faithfully keep the Eleventh Commandment—
I will not allow my mind to harm me through knight in shining armor fantasies.
I will find someone to hold me accountable to this pledge
and to God's plan for my life.
I will wait for God's Boaz, and I will be honest with myself
about the Bozos I meet along the way.
I will become a woman worth waiting for as I await God's best for me. –JMK[4]

BECOMING A LADY OF CONTENTMENT

- Do you have a spiritual monitor? Are you a spiritual monitor? (Read Proverbs 28:23 and Hebrews 3:13.) Are you intimidated by the prospect of this role in a friend's life? Why?

- Review the methods of defrauding by a guy and by yourself. (Read First Thessalonians 4:6.)

- A contented woman has the ability to lay down the terrible burden of always needing life on her terms. Are you a contented woman? (Read Judges 21:25; Luke 1:38; Matthew 26:39.)

- Pride is an excessively high opinion of what one deserves. Do you struggle with pride's control of your desires? (Read Proverbs 13:10, 16:18, 29:23; Jeremiah 5:3; James 4:1-2.)

- Does toe-tapping, nail-biting, "I'm a quarter past thirty years old" thinking rob you of contentment? What limits God from acting on your behalf? (Read Matthew 6:27; Isaiah 30:18, 64:4.)

- Discuss the quote: "Expectations are premeditated resentment."

- Discuss the: Ten vs. Five Theory. Have you been enhancing your discontentment as a single because of your fantasies and unrealistic expectations?

- After finishing this study—consider examining the list of the comparisons between the Proverbs 31 woman and Ruth.

ENDNOTES

1. Anne Lamott, *Blue Shoes* (New York: Riverhead Books, 2002), 136.

2. John W. Gardner, Facebook post, July 22, 2012.

3. Lloyd Ogilvie, *The Bush Is Still Burning* (Waco, TX: Word Books, 1980), 159.

4. Kendall, *A Man Worth Waiting For*, 207.

Chapter 9

LADY OF CONVICTION

On the eve of her wedding day, Cindy, a Lady of Conviction, wrote the following poem to her bridegroom:

Dear Sweetheart,

For many years I sought to find my most perfect mate, but all that ever resulted from my search were shattered dreams, a broken heart, and what seemed to be an endless wait. I wanted to find God's very best, but first He had to teach me that in His loving hands, I must solely rest.

So one evening I prayed, "God, just as You put Adam to sleep until the perfect one for him, he was ready to meet; so put me and my desires to sleep until I too am ready to know the one You have chosen for me."

From that time forward, God gave me a peace. And although others came into my life, God protected my heart and spared me from more strife. Then when God knew that in His hands I had placed my heart, He brought you into my life, and I was history from the start.

My dear friends who know me well perhaps see tomorrow as a miraculous day. For they have known me and all my picky ways. Once while in the dorm, A.M. came into my room and asked me just exactly what I was looking for in a man. I ran to my diary and pulled out a list of 30 qualities I was looking for and on which I would insist.

As I read each trait one by one, dear A.M. looked at me; she was very stunned. After pondering the list she said with a nod, "Well, Cindy, looks like you'll have to marry God." Well, God you are not, but my heaven on earth you are. God heard my prayers and answered them in the most perfect way with you.

I have no unanswered questions, no doubts, no hesitations, no reservations. You are my Prince Charming, my knight in shining armor, my gift from the sea, my gift from God. —Cindy Jordan Feldewerth

Does it seem too unrealistic for today's woman to set her sights on a knight in shining armor? Was Cindy just an idealist who got lucky and found a man who satisfied her list of "30 traits"? A single friend (a modern Ruth) wrote a letter in which she admitted that her high ideals often made her feel like the "Lone Ranger." She said, "So often I meet women who don't want to go the deeper, more radical route of separation from our culture in seeking after God's standards." Do we lower our standards because we seem out of step with all our peers? Does the woman in Proverbs 31 seem obsolete? Maybe for the "cosmopolitan" woman she is obsolete, but not for the Lady of Conviction. God has the best in hand for those who seek Him.

Ruth's choice to wait for God's best resulted in her union with a Boaz rather than a Bozo. Ruth not only married a man who was a "pillar of strength" (Boaz), but she also was blessed by the privilege of bearing a son (Obed) who would be part of the lineage of Jesus Christ. Ruth's wise choices resulted in her experiencing God's overwhelming goodness.

DAMAGED GOODS

Ruth did not allow the past influences of a heathen culture to keep her from setting new standards and making wise choices for her life that would honor God. Ruth could have allowed herself to remain within a destructive family cycle that moved against God's standards. She could have given up on a godly lifestyle by assuming she was doomed as "damaged goods." But she didn't. She chose, instead, to break her family's sin cycle and establish a new godly cycle.

Ruth did not allow the past influences of a heathen culture to keep her from setting new standards and making wise choices for her life that would honor God.

After becoming a Christian, Jackie found herself ashamed of her lack of a proper upbringing. She says this:

I knew I had been forgiven for the past, but I often wrestled with the feelings of being damaged goods. I found myself envying other girls who were from godly homes and great heritages, spiritually. Whenever I would be introduced to a wonderful Christian guy, I would immediately think, "I'm not good enough."

This was exactly how I felt when I first met my husband. He had asked Jesus to take control of his life at the young age of eleven. He went to church faithfully; he never smoked, drank, or fooled around sexually. His high standards were very intimidating to me. Throughout the years of our friendship, I knew he would never date me because of my imperfect past and ungodly family. Was I in for a surprise!

As I continued to make choices to break the ungodly influences of my past, the Lord was working on bringing Ken and me together as a team for His glory. Like David, I thought, *"Who am I, O Sovereign Lord, and what is my family, that You have brought me this far?"* (2 Sam. 7:18 NIV).

Ungodly cycles can be broken. Your destiny is not something that is left to chance or fate; it is the product of wise choices.

DESTINY—CHANCE OR CHOICE?

Do you think your ideals and standards are too high? Do you feel the pressure to compromise and settle for the generic version of life? Ruth lived in an era that was exactly like modern America. Judges 21:25 describes the era in which she lived: *"In those days there was no king in Israel; everyone did what was right in his own eyes."* We too live in a culture where it seems that no one fears God and people just "do their own thing."

You, like Ruth, will be greatly affected by your choices. Ruth's wise choices allowed her to break a godless family cycle and begin a new cycle that the Word of God triumphantly records. God has not changed—and neither have men. The high standards in God's Word are not irrelevant, but completely applicable to finding God's best for your life. Choices, guided by your convictions rather than by chance, determine your destiny. How wise have your decisions been in the past in regard to relating to and dating men? Have you made some poor choices that you can see were the result of your own lack of proper convictions in the areas of love, sex, and dating? Your present choices will affect the rest of your life in this delicate area that is often a collision course—male/female relating.

You cannot make good choices without proper, biblical convictions. Don't carelessly leave your dating/relating standards to chance. Too much depends on your decisions in this area. A stanza from the song "Guard Your Heart" by Jon Mohr captures this warning:

> *The human heart is easily swayed*
> *and often betrayed*
> *at the hand of emotion.*
> *We dare not leave the outcome to chance;*
> *we must choose in advance*
> *or live in agony,*
> *such needless tragedy.*

From the beginning of time, God has shown His own people exactly what course they should take to avoid needless tragedy. A passage of Scripture that clearly states the reality of our own choices of happiness or misery is Deuteronomy 30:15-20. Remember that the media, music, literature, teachers, and peers often oppose the godly choices that you might want to make.

While reading the wonderful book *Marriable: Taking the Desperate Out of Dating,* I came upon a list that made me smile, because it confirmed yet again that Boazes exist in the 21st century. It delineates well what a Boaz acts like in a dating situation:

A gentleman:

- never asks her out for a date less than three days before said date.

- always picks her up at the front door for the date.

- isn't late picking her up.

- doesn't complain when she isn't ready when he gets there.

- has a plan for the evening and is prepared for changes in weather and/or activity.

- never asks her to pay for the date.

- doesn't check out other women when he's with her.

- doesn't stare at her assorted body parts.

- always calls after the date to tell her he had a good time.

- doesn't apologize for being a man.[1]

As a Lady of Conviction, you will want to stay alert to recognize these acts of respect by a guy who's interested in dating you. If he's oblivious to these standards of behavior, your convictions can't *make* him respect you; but they can serve to guard your heart from further attachment to one who is less than a Boaz.

STANDARD-BEARER

May we go back to the basics for just a moment? What is a conviction, and how does one develop biblical convictions? A conviction is a standard that serves as a springboard for your choices. Consider where your standards, in the area of relating and dating, originated. Are your standards based more on Hollywood's terms of love and romance, or have you allowed God's Holy Word to shape your perspective?

The Lady of Conviction gives the Lord permission to renew her mind on a daily basis. She spends time searching the Word of God for standards that will guide her safely to God's best. She has made a significant choice as a godly woman. She has surrendered her mind to a new persuasion: God's perspective on love and romance. The convictions that she establishes, based on the Word, allow her to resist being squeezed into the mold of this world. She is a non-conformist in a biblical sense, as in Romans 12:2 (NIV) which says:

*Do not conform any longer to the pattern of this world, but be transformed by the renewing of your mind. Then **you will be able to test and approve** what God's will is—His good, pleasing and perfect will.*

Notice the words *test* and *approve;* your convictions (whether Hollywood-based or Bible-based) gauge your ability to "test and approve" the relationships you've had or will have.

Through Jesus' strength, you can stand firm, unwavering, as you wait for His best.

If you want to live by God's standards for love, sex, and dating, you must prepare yourself for the inevitable resistance that standard-bearers face. When you live by your convictions, many of your friends will consider you unrealistic. Some of your girlfriends may even think you are stubbornly opinionated. Facing such opposition from the people you love is not easy, but the Lord will give you the grace to refuse to compromise. A true standard-bearer wants to be a vanguard in a movement. Through Jesus' strength, you can stand firm, unwavering, as you wait for His best.

The woman without the high ideals that the Word of God sets forth leaves her choices to chance. She tends to end up with a Bozo rather than a Boaz because she cannot measure accurately the man behind the "makeup."

Since most biblical convictions are in opposition to all the propaganda from Hollywood, relatively few, even among Christians, hold to these standards. This harsh reality is revealed throughout the Word:

> *You are like unfaithful wives, flirting with the glamour of this world, and never realizing that to be the world's lover means becoming the enemy of God! Anyone who deliberately chooses to love the world is thereby making himself God's enemy. Or do you think what the scriptures have to say about this is a mere formality?* (James 4:4-5 PNT)

When you pass up dates with certain guys because you know they do not measure up to God's standards, then you have taken seriously your commitment not to oppose God. If your friends pressure and oppose you, ask the Lord for the strength to be more concerned with being His friend and not His enemy through compromising standards.

In America, government agencies regulate the standards of the food that you consume on a daily basis. For example, meat is subject to federal regulation of its grade, weight, and quality. How much more significant than ground beef (even prime rib) is the man with whom you hope to share the rest of your life? Such consideration and evaluation cannot be obtained through a glance or chance encounter at the "meet" counter. A lifelong relationship demands the highest standards of regulation. There are men breathing on this planet today who can handle such scrutiny and be found "worth waiting for."

AVOIDING BOZOS

What is a Bozo? A Bozo is a guy whose outward appearance is a façade. It is hard to discern who he really is because of the "makeup and costume" he wears. What he appears to be physically, socially, and even spiritually is just a performance. A Bozo is a counterfeit Boaz.

It is possible to avoid such a clown. Your standards and convictions will help you recognize the difference. The remainder of this chapter accentuates the genuine Boaz. Concentrating on the real thing will make the Bozos more apparent.

Before any girl accepts her first date, she should have established in her heart and mind a biblical alternative to Hollywood's dating style. As a prerequisite to every date, you should examine your motive (elaborated in the chapter on contentment). Are you going out with this guy because you haven't had a date in years? Are you going out with someone who may not really be a Christian because you think a date—even with a Bozo—is better than no date at all?

Many women spend time with guys who do not really care for them. They would rather waste an evening with a Bozo than face another lonely night in a dateless condition. Some women even give up their biblical convictions in order to get a date with a certain guy. Do you feel as though you allow your dating schedule to determine your personal worth? Many single women are prisoners of the world's dating syndrome. They equate their self-worth with how many dates they had last month.

THE STUD PURSE

Several years ago, a single woman from New York City sent me a gift. When I first saw it, I was puzzled. Inside the box was a vivid red purse embossed with bright white capital letters spelling out *STUD*. What an odd gift!

Then I read her note and it clarified her intention. Ana had sent this purse for me to use as a visual aid when teaching gals about the local Bozo guys. I began to do just that. On one trip, I found the purse in my suitcase with a glossy brochure melted right onto the purse. I tried in vain to carefully remove the paper that had melted into the plastic, and what remained was a big black mess. I groaned, thinking that my great visual was ruined. But after looking at the black stain for a few moments, the Lord showed me that the stain on my STUD purse was perfect.

You see, the black, messy scar was on the *back* side of the purse, whereas the word *STUD* had not been ruined. So now I actually had a new and improved visual aid. The next time I used the STUD purse when teaching "How to Avoid a Bozo Guy," I showed the perfect front of the purse, displaying STUD. Then I turned it over and showed the gals the black, messy scar on the back!

When I use this visual, I tell the singles that "STUD guys" too often leave terrible scars on the hearts of gals. The gals go from laughing to groaning as some of them reflect on the Bozo guys who have already hurt their hearts. I now travel with the purse wrapped in tissue paper to protect this poignant visual aid!

To avoid marrying a Bozo, one needs to have a clear picture of the difference between God's best—a Boaz—and the all too often "attractive" counterfeit—a Bozo. A Lady of Conviction knows the distinct differences between the two. She is not easily distracted by the studs in her world. By the way, most gals can give you the name of the studs in their world.

Across America, you can find females of all ages swooning whenever a stud so much as smiles at them in the hallway en route to his next class. You can hear the girl sharing breathlessly with her best friend, "He spoke to me after English class!" This swooning girl is convinced that Mr. Stud is interested in her because he spoke to her for almost a whole minute. But let's be sober here! The problem with studs is how they can potentially scar you.

When you're in awe of a guy like this, you're more vulnerable to being taken advantage of physically. The stud knows that you're "swooning and crushing" on him, and he is more than willing to give you the attention you're hungry for—which often results in *you*, the swooning one, getting escorted to the No Zone by the stud. This may seem cruel or even exaggerated, but I have been listening for four decades to thousands of gals who have been taken advantage of, used, and then disposed of.

Have you dated more Bozos than Boazes? If your answer is yes, you may need to develop higher ideals. A very attractive and popular high school girl was challenged to develop a list of biblical dating standards and to put them into practice. She carried a copy of those standards in her wallet for five years. Thus she dated more Boazes than Bozos because her convictions helped her clearly see the type of guys with whom she was relating and ultimately dating. Do you carry God's standards for dating in your heart as well as in your wallet?

One Auburn University graduate left school with not only a diploma but also a very specific list of the qualities she was looking for in a future mate. See if her list contains any of the qualities you are looking for in Mr. Right:

- Spirit-controlled Christian (see Eph. 5:18).

- Jesus is #1 in his life, not just an ornament (see Mark 12:30).

- Broken; understands how to rely totally upon Jesus (see Phil. 4:13).

- Ministry minded; wherever he is, he is available (see 1 Cor. 4:2 NIV).

- Motivator; man of vision, concerned about lost souls (see Rom. 10:14).

- Sensitive spirit; in tune to the needs of others (see Gal. 6:2).

- Understands the awesome responsibility of a husband to his wife (see Eph. 5:25-31).

- Humble enough to be a disciple (teachable) and able to disciple others (see Matt. 28:19-20).

- Man of prayer; he knows the key to success is his private time with God (see Col. 4:2).

- Family man; he desires to have children and raise them properly for God's glory (see Prov. 22:6).

In 2007, I was getting ready to write another book and I decided to send out a questionnaire to a few hundred guys I knew. (Having worked with professional athletes for fifteen years at that time, I knew a lot of guys.) The responses I received were so touching and inspiring. One of my conclusions after reading them was this: Deep in their hearts, men know God's ideals. They have the desire to be better guys, not Bozo guys. Guys need girls who have standards and convictions to remind them of those ideals deep in their hearts.

> *They show that the requirements of the law are written on their hearts, their consciences also bearing witness, and their thoughts now accusing, now even defending them* (Romans 2:15 NIV).

A Lady of Conviction can be a gentle but strong reminder of the God-given conscience that nudges young men to stop acting like Bozos.

While waiting for my time to speak for the Fellowship of Christian Athletes at the University of South Carolina, a young man approached me. With the biggest smile, he said, "I just want you to know that I read your book."

My stunned reply was, "Really? You read *Lady in Waiting*?"

"Yes ma'am, I have," he said. "When my girlfriend broke up with me, she handed me *Lady in Waiting* and said, 'This is why I'm breaking up with you.'"

He went on to tell me how angry and in shock he was as he returned to his dorm room and threw down the book. Later on, and somewhat calmed down, he picked up the book and started to read it, out of curiosity. Then he said to me, "You know the best part of reading that book? Now I know what a *woman* worth waiting for is like."

His final words put a huge smile on my face. That was when he said, "All the guys in my suite also read it."

A Lady of Conviction can be a gentle but strong reminder of the God-given conscience that nudges young men to stop acting like Bozos.

Clear standards for dating and relating will guard you against compromise and making wrong choices out of sudden emotion rather than a God-directed will. These guidelines for your dating friendships will keep God as your focus rather than allowing the guy to become the focus (idol). Clear standards coupled with accountability to a sister in Christ will help you walk in the convictions you establish. To guard you against haphazard meetings or just the "WFs" (weird feelings) in your heart, you need standards for which you will be accountable.

PAINFUL DISCLAIMER

A disclaimer (or an additional note) that we would like to include at this point is not to simplify the reason so many women are attracted to Bozos. The issue of standards is most relevant, but may seem simplistic. We acknowledge that some women find it difficult to raise their standards and change their patterns because they are still entangled with the past.

Unresolved conflicts with a father, a brother, or an ex-boyfriend may overshadow and control the attraction to Bozos. In this case, we suggest a possible date fast, a period of time during which you refrain from accepting another date until you can sort out some of the unresolved conflicts from the past. This method has been used by many single women who have been entangled with old dating patterns. During the "date fast," they find time to search for new ways of relating and dating biblically.

If you have already spent time with the Lord establishing dating/relating standards, then you will receive affirmation through the following material. If you have been letting your dating routine be controlled by chance rather than biblical choice, consider not accepting another date until you have nailed down your convictions. Too much is at stake.

Once you have set dating standards and understand the significance of a constant motive check (daily bringing the flutters in your heart to the Lord), you are ready to consider other guidelines for successful dating and relating.

WEDDING DAY CHAINS

"Here comes the bride all dressed in…chains!" Hey, wasn't that supposed to be "all dressed in white"? The last word in the chorus was changed to "chains," not because the bride is marrying a member of a motorcycle gang, but because she made the unwise choice of marrying an unbeliever. The chains symbolize what she has to look forward to as a believer married to an unbeliever. The Word of God speaks clearly about a partnership with an unbeliever. A common verse used for this conviction is Second Corinthians 6:14-17, but there is a more poignant message for the one who wavers in this conviction in Joshua.

But if you turn away and ally yourselves with the survivors of these nations that remain among you and if you intermarry with them and associate with them, then you may be sure that the Lord your God will no longer drive out these nations before you. Instead, they will become snares and traps for you, whips on your backs and thorns in your eyes, until you perish from this good land, which the Lord your God has given you (Joshua 23:12-13 NIV).

One would be foolish to disobey God in the area of marrying an unbeliever.

When a single woman experiences a prolonged period of datelessness, loneliness tempts her to compromise her conviction concerning dating a growing Christian. Her dateless state may pressure her to surrender to the temptation of dating an unbeliever. She may justify such a date in the guise of being a witness for Jesus. Many single women have been trapped emotionally with an unbeliever when it all began with "missionary dating."

Ponder this: every unbelieving marriage partner arrived as an unbeliever on the first date. As trite as it may seem, every date is a potential mate. Avoid dating an unbeliever.

Many women want so desperately to date that the only qualification they have for the guy is that he goes to church. Every Sunday, people attend church to appease God or to satisfy a religious urge. You must set a higher standard and resist dating a guy who is not growing in his intimacy with Christ.

THE MAN WORTH WAITING FOR

How would you describe the ideal man? A group of sharp women were asked to describe a man worth waiting for, and all of them immediately replied: spiritual leader. One woman expounded on this quality in her unique way: "I want a guy who enjoys talking about Jesus in such a way that it reveals his obvious, bursting love for Him." Too many guys want to talk about Jesus for 60 seconds and their car or job or latest toy for the rest of the evening. One woman shared a verse that she thought his life should reflect: Psalm 73:25, which says, *"Whom have I in heaven but You* [the Lord]? *And besides You, I desire nothing on earth."* Do such spiritual men exist? Yes, but they are exceptions and not the rule. Their appearance requires waiting on the part of the recipient.

SUPERFICIALITY OF APPEARANCE

Growing up, I noticed that I was always attracted to guys with dark hair and dark eyes; whereas I had friends who were attracted to guys with blonde hair and blue eyes. These attractions were a reflection of not only our personal preferences but also a level of immaturity. The ideal guy each of us had in mind was external; the idea was limited to his physical characteristics. Whenever I hear gals describing guys as being so cute or so hot, I always ask, "What is his heart like? How does he treat those around him?" God's Word speaks loudly to the superficiality of appearance.

> But the Lord said to Samuel, "Do not consider his appearance or his height, for I have rejected him. The Lord does not look at the things man looks at. Man looks at the outward appearance, but the Lord looks at the heart" (1 Samuel 16:7 NIV).

When my husband and I first met, he was *not* struck with love at first sight. In fact, his first thought was, "What in the world just walked into the Bible study!" I had just moved to South Florida from California. I looked like the wildest hippie, with my very short dress and wire-rimmed glasses, long crazy hair, and the biggest Bible ever carried to a youth meeting!

My first thought when I saw my husband was, "This can't be the youth leader. He must be the pastor!" My husband's hair was very short and he was all dressed up, wearing a tie, and leading the youth Bible study. My youth leader in California didn't own a tie and had long hair. If my husband and I had made our future decisions about each other based on appearance, we would not have married. He was blonde and blue-eyed—the opposite of what I normally was attracted to. I had dark hair and dark eyes—the opposite of his high school sweetheart.

Before considering the specific qualities found in a Boaz, one should deal with certain physical stereotypes. Whether you have been looking for a guy who is a bronzed, blue-eyed blond (B.B.B.) or is tall, dark, and handsome (T.D.H.), you need to surrender your desires to the Lord. Everyone has certain preferences. But such a mindset needs to be given to Jesus. Too many single women have missed wonderful treasures in godly guys because the treasure was not encased in a B.B.B. or T.D.H.

The Lord will probably not require you to date a guy who repulses you physically. But you need to be open to guys who do not fit your desired stereotype. Too often a guy may satisfy your eyesight, but leave your heart empty and still longing. Remember, after a few years that bronzed, blue-eyed blond can be transformed into a pale, bald guy with bifocals on those gorgeous eyes.

A famous actress told a Christian psychologist that her five husbands had all been attractive outside (they were all B.B.B.s or T.D.H.s), but rotten on the inside. How many women, after the honeymoon is over, feel like they married a stranger? How many newlyweds are disillusioned by their mate's behavior within a few months of marriage? Most marriage counseling problems have their roots in personality problems—not physiques.

BOAZ—PROFILE OF A MAN WORTH WAITING FOR

The Book of Ruth gives not only the story of a Lady in Waiting, but also the profile of a knight in shining armor. From the first mention of this man

Boaz (chapter 2…read and re-read), you begin to notice special qualities that distinguish a Boaz from a Bozo.

You want to marry someone for the qualities he possesses now, not for the qualities you hope he will develop. The most common mistake made by marriage partners is marrying someone they intend to change. Since it is nearly impossible to change a person, you will want to set standards of dating, or of building friendships, with men who are characterized by the following qualities. A single woman can sidestep a lifetime of tragedy by seriously considering these characteristics in a prospective steady date.

- *Puts the needs of others ahead of his own.* This man accepts people just the way they are, loving others even when his love is not returned. He will continue to love someone because of his commitment to that person, not because of how he feels.

Do nothing from selfishness or empty conceit, but with humility of mind regard one another as more important than yourselves; do not merely look out for your own personal interests, but also for the interests of others (Philippians 2:3-4).

- *Rejoices in his relationship with Christ.* You don't have to ask this man if he is a Christian. His joy in the Lord is evident in his life.

These things I have spoken to you so that My joy may be in you, and that your joy may be made full (John 15:11).

- *Maintains proper relationships.* This man seeks a good relationship with everyone—from his friends to his parents. He listens to differing perspectives without feeling threatened. He has the strength to back off from a fight. He works to forgive wrongs done to him and seeks to make his own offenses right. He will not hold a grudge.

Pursue peace with all men… (Hebrews 12:14).

- *Refuses to jump ahead of God's timing.* He is not so eager to be something, do something, or have something that he cannot wait on God's timing. He chooses against impulsiveness so he may be in the exact center of God's will.

Rest in the Lord and wait patiently for Him... (Psalm 37:7).

- *Seeks to meet the practical needs of others.* He is not so self-absorbed that he cannot make time for the needy. He is interested in the welfare of others and is willing to give his time, money, and energy for their benefit.

Be kind to one another, tender-hearted... (Ephesians 4:32).

- *Stands for what is right.* He hates anything contrary to God's holy character. He is known as a man of integrity by those with whom he works.

There will be...glory and honor and peace to everyone who does good... (Romans 2:9-10).

- *Follows through on his God-given responsibilities.* He uses the talents God has given him and realizes that "he + Jesus = adequacy for any God-given job." He is neither overconfident nor absorbed with feelings of inferiority. He is not a dreamer, wishing for more ability, but a diligent steward of the talents he has been given. This man is dependable and stays with even a difficult task until it is completed.

Now it is required that those who have been given a trust must prove faithful (1 Corinthians 4:2 NIV).

- *Understands the importance of feelings and emotions.* Some women may find themselves attracted to a demanding man, assuming that his dominance will be their security. Other women may marry a doormat they can dominate, but inevitably end up despising the man's weakness. A gentle man is the best of both; he takes the initiative to lead but tempers it with gentle responses toward the other's feelings.

So, as those who have been chosen of God, holy and beloved, put on a heart of compassion, kindness, humility, gentleness and patience (Colossians 3:12).

- *Flees temptations to compromise.* This man refuses to be in situations that are sensual, immoral, or impure. He does not entertain friendships that lead to drunkenness or carousing. He avoids talk that could cause strife or jealousy. This man does not allow a temper to control him or anger to destroy him.

Like a city that is broken into and without walls is a man who has no control over his spirit (Proverbs 25:28).

These qualities are not unrealistic ideals. When a man follows Jesus, the Holy Spirit works these into his life. In fact, you can read this list again and match the fruit of the Spirit with the appropriate characteristic: "*But the fruit of the Spirit is love, joy, peace, patience, kindness, goodness, faithfulness, gentleness, self-control; against such things there is no law*" (Gal. 5:22-23).

None of the men you date will have all these qualities perfected. All of us are at differing levels of maturity. A man of God is one who works toward being conformed to the character of Christ. But be careful when a quality of God's Spirit is completely missing in a man's life and he is unwilling to deal with it before marriage. Realize that if character is absent before the wedding ceremony, it will be missing after the wedding ceremony and cause considerable problems during marriage.

Be careful when a quality of God's Spirit is completely missing in a man's life and he is unwilling to deal with it before marriage.

Was Boaz, Ruth's knight, the last man of godly character, or was he just one of many? We are convinced that God still grooms Boazes for His daughters today. This does not mean a guy has to be perfect in order for you to go out with him. It does mean that he needs to be growing in Christlikeness by the enabling power of the Holy Spirit before you start to date him.

Do you want to marry a knight in shining armor? Then set your standards high. To be married to a man who loves the Lord and wants to serve Him is one of life's highest privileges. It is worth whatever wait, whatever cost. Nail down your convictions and refuse to compromise by dating men who are not controlled by God's Holy Spirit. These standards will stand guard over the castle of your heart. Proverbs 4:23 (NIV) says, *"Above all else, guard your heart, for it is the wellspring of life."*

Without high standards, even Christian gals are easily seduced

I want to share a ghastly but sobering story that impacted me so deeply that it needs to be shared with every single female I encounter (in all ages and stages of singleness). First, they need to grasp this reality: a guy doesn't treat a gal with special deference just because he claims to "love" her. A guy's special treatment of a particular gal is part of his hormone-throbbing agenda. He is (whether consciously or subconsciously) on the hunt for a gal who will join him in the adventure of exploring the No Zone (sexual sin)!

Just as guys are addicted to sports and video games, they are also driven by the Number One need of *all* males—*sex!* This is in their wiring, and this hyped-up sexual society has not encouraged them to bulk up the muscle of self-control!

So here is the *must share* story I saw on "Oprah" one day. Two teenagers, a boy and girl, and their mothers were guests on the show. (DO NOT skip this story just because you are not a teen...the reality continues through all of one's singleness.) These teens were willing to discuss on TV their "being ready to have intercourse." The couple had dated almost a year, beginning at age fourteen. During that time they had progressed through the No Zone, and now felt their love justified their readiness to go "all the way."

The two mothers voiced their opinions. One mother was appalled at the suggestion and the other mother felt it was the natural progression of love. The teens continued to defend what they "felt" about each other and how their love made intercourse seem so right.

Besides the million-plus TV viewers listening to the teens, there was an expert sex therapist on the show. I couldn't wait to hear what this "expert" would say in response. I was literally on the edge of my seat.

The doctor leaned forward and directed her question to the young boy. "After you two finally have sex, how long will you continue to date your girlfriend?"

In the brief moment before the boy replied, the camera shifted to his girlfriend, showing her adoring gaze toward him. She obviously anticipated his loving reply. Yet without another moment of hesitation, the boy said, "Maybe six more months."

Of course, the camera caught the shock on the girl's face. The wise doctor immediately directed her next question to the girl: "Did his answer surprise you?"

"Yes!" the poor girl replied, clearly stunned. "I thought because we love each other our love is forever."

This fifteen-year-old girl did not know the hard truth that "guys play at love to get sex." Then the doctor asked the girl, "Are you now reconsidering going all the way with him?"

The teen girl quickly replied, "Yes, I am reconsidering."

Her reply brought a huge round of applause from the audience. And I sat in my front room screaming: "Don't do it, girlfriend. Sex is not love!"

This is not just the "foolishness of young love"! I can't even count the number of foolish, older, single women I have met who think they are smarter than God's standard (see 1 Thess. 4:3-8; 1 Cor. 6:18-19) and actually think they get a pass on this area because of their circumstances of prolonged singleness!

There is a heartbreaking story in God's Word (see 2 Sam. 13:1-16) where a prince declared his love for a particular virgin named Tamar. He actually stated that he was "lovesick" for her. (Note: love does not make you sick—crushing and lusting make you sick!) After Prince Amnon got what he wanted sexually, by raping this innocent girl, the Scripture recounts a most painful outcome:

> *Then Amnon hated her with intense hatred. In fact, he hated her more than he had loved her. Amnon said, "Get up and get out!"* (2 Samuel 13:15 NIV)

I can say with certainty that most gals will never face something as horrendous as rape, but I can also say that plenty of our girls will encounter guys who would attempt to seduce them with words. This seduction terminology needs to be exposed. Some of the most common lines Bozo guys use are: "I have never felt this way about anybody," or, "You're different from any other girl in my life."

Guys consistently utilize these ploys to seduce and *emotionally rape* gals who are vulnerable to such flattery!

BECOMING A LADY OF CONVICTION

- Write out your convictions for the kind of guys you will date and the Scriptures where you found those qualities. Why did you select these particular convictions?

- What is the problem with just dating guys who are good, but who are not Christians? What is the difference between a good man who goes to church and a growing Christian man? What difference would it make in marriage?

- If the wait becomes hard and you meet someone who loves you, but has a glaring character flaw, what do you sacrifice if you marry him? Look through each of the characteristics found in the Man Worth Waiting For section and determine what would be lost in your marriage if that quality was missing in your husband and the father of your children.

- Put a check beside each of the following characteristics that *you* can change in your husband after marriage:

_____ Unwillingness to communicate (see Prov. 14:10)

_____ Dominating ego (see Rom. 12:3)

_____ Bad temper (see James 1:19-20)

_____ Argumentative tendencies (see Prov. 20:3)

_____ Difficulty in apologizing (see Eph. 4:32)

_____ Bad language (see Eph. 5:4)

_____ Unwillingness to be involved with church (see Heb. 10:24-25)

_____ Inability to keep a job (see 1 Tim. 5:8)

_____ Jealousy (see 1 Cor. 13:4)

_____ Self-centeredness (see 2 Cor. 5:15)

_____ Depression (see 2 Cor. 4:16)

_____ Unwillingness to give (see 2 Cor. 9:7)

_____ Always "going with the guys" (see 1 Cor. 15:33)

_____ Wandering eyes (see 1 Thess. 4:2-7)

_____ Lying (see Eph. 4:25)

_____ Immaturity (see Eph. 4:15)

_____ Workaholic tendencies (see 1 Tim. 6:7-11)

- What does the Bible say about these qualities in reference to godliness?

ENDNOTE

1. Hayley and Michael DiMarco, *Marriable: Taking the Desperate Out of Dating* (Grand Rapids, MI: Baker Publishing Group, 2005), 127.

Chapter 10

LADY OF PATIENCE

Janis and Linda were longtime friends and roommates. Inside their hall closet hung two sizes of every color of bridesmaid dress imaginable. "Well," they would say with a laugh, "we have been bridesmaids at the weddings of many friends, but we are still here, holding out for the man God has for each of us!" Linda often added, "One thing I do know, when I walk down that aisle in white I want 'Great Is Thy Faithfulness' to be the procession song."

Although their ability to joke in the midst of their prolonged singleness is admirable, one has to wonder how an older woman can be patient when there appears to be no end to the waiting in sight. Waiting isn't easy when you are young, and it can be terribly hard as you get older.

God demonstrated His faithfulness in a special way to these two close single friends who chose to wait for His best, whether they married or not. He allowed each of their princes to appear within weeks of each other. Linda and Janis rejoiced in the faithfulness of God as they planned their weddings and then participated in each other's wedding ceremony. They witnessed God's faithfulness in marriage as in singleness because they waited on His perfect timing for their future.

Was the wait easy? No. Was the wait worth it? Many years of marriage and six children later, the two friends answer with a resounding, "Praise God. Yes, the wait was worth it!"

Take courage, single friend. You are not alone in your wait; neither are you alone in the feelings and struggles you encounter. Many godly women have waited and won. Many women have lost hope and compromised. Wait patiently and win triumphantly the future your Father has planned for you. It will always be designed with you in mind and is worth being patient to discover.

Ruth was a wonderful example of a Lady of Patience. Ruth did not allow her circumstances or lack of male companionship to cause her to be impatient. Instead she concentrated on developing companionship with her heavenly Father and chose to let Him bring a husband to her if He saw fit. Concern over the ticking of her "biological clock" did not make her fearful of the future. Instead she concentrated on being a lady of character, not on getting a man. She took one day at a time, knowing that God was not bound by circumstances or her age. She used the wait to become the woman God wanted her to be. At the end of this personal preparation God chose to provide her with a husband. In Ruth 4:13, we see the end to their love story: *So Boaz took Ruth, and she became his wife...."*

WHY IS WAITING SO HARD?

If God is faithful, why is it so easy to lose patience? Why is it so hard to wait? Why is it easier to settle for less than God's best? Fear is a huge hindrance to waiting. You may fear that your biological clock is ticking away and God has not noticed. You may fear, with every wedding you attend, that soon you will no longer have any single friends. You might feel that you better marry this "okay fella" who just proposed because he's pretty good and you fear you may not find another. Or possibly you fear loneliness and a lifetime of eating by yourself and of going to a church filled with people, only to sit alone.

Fear is a huge hindrance to waiting.

Fear is an internal pressure. There are external pressures as well. Society pushes single women to grab for marriage because of a male shortage. Your parents want grandchildren, and your cousins want to know, "What's wrong with you?" You feel like you don't fit in with the youth any longer, but you can't very well go to the young marrieds' functions at church (where your friends now attend). If that isn't enough, a knowledge of statistics on singleness can finish you off:

> Marriage patterns in the United States revealed: white college-educated women born in the mid-50s who are still single at thirty have a 20% chance of marrying. By the age of 35, the odds drop to 5%. Forty-year-olds are more likely to be killed by a terrorist than the minuscule 2.6% probability of tying the knot.[1]

How encouraging! The world is attacking a single woman's confidence as the enemy discourages her hopes through fear. These pressures often provoke single women to take more initiative rather than patiently wait for God's best.

Is *Wait* a Cuss Word?

The apprenticeship of patience is not an option for our future security and happiness. Having to *wait* for things you really want develops your self-control. This will bless absolutely every aspect of your future. A parenting pattern of instant gratification for whatever a child wants will undermine the child's chance to become patient.

The apprenticeship of patience is not an option for our future security and happiness. Having to wait for things you really want develops your self-control.

Is the four-letter word *wait* like a cuss word to you? Whenever I speak to a teen, college, or singles gathering and mention this four-letter word *wait,*

I always hear sighing and groaning from the gals. Would you be one of the members of the chorus of groaners? How patient are you?

Waiting is a prerequisite for God's best. *And if God's best is a husband, then waiting on God is the best plan for finding a Boaz.* Conversely, impatience is the easiest way to find a Bozo. When I speak about patience and waiting, I always ask this question: "What is worse than waiting?" As the gals ponder their answers, I blurt out my answer: "Wishing you had!" I have spent decades counseling all those who *wished* they had waited for their Boaz.

> *Since ancient times no one has heard, no ear has perceived, no eye has seen any God besides you, who acts on behalf of those who **wait** for Him* (Isaiah 64:4 NIV).

So in your training as a Lady of Patience, remember this extraordinary quality of our God: *He is spurred on by our waiting!*

CONSEQUENCES OF IMPATIENCE

There are grave consequences for the single woman who does not choose to develop patience and wait on God's timing. Society is full of heartbreaking examples. Some end in divorce; others end in an emotional separation that causes the husband and wife to merely live under the same roof. Some leave precious children damaged by the insecurity and fear that an unhealthy marriage produces. The personal loneliness and hurt that these lifestyles bring can be indescribably painful. God did not intend a woman to have to live like that.

Impatience to find a man can cause a woman to argue about her "right" to date a man who is not godly, maybe not even a Christian. In Joshua 23:12-14, the Lord warns His people not to marry unbelievers. God knows that an ungodly husband will end up being *"snares and traps for you, whips on your backs and thorns in your eyes…"* (Josh. 23:13 NIV). Many young women argue that they are just dating, not marrying, an unbeliever. But remember— in our society, does anyone ever marry someone he or she never dated? *Every date is a potential mate.*

VULNERABILITY TO MISSIONARY DATING

Patience was the red carpet that Ruth walked down to receive God's best for her: Boaz, a man worth waiting for. I have seen countless women miss the red carpet to God's best because of their inability to wait. Impatience in everyday life may seem like a minor flaw, but patience is critical for you to receive God's best. And beware! The longer you're dateless, the more vulnerable you become to impatience in waiting for "Mr. Right."

Dating was never meant to be a mission field; but many a young (and not-so-young) Christian woman is tempted to venture into that perilous field. I have received so many letters from single girls who want to know if it is okay to date a nonbeliever. They defend the guy they are interested in by describing how wonderful he is. They write pages describing this "Mr. Right" and conclude with something like, "Well, the only fault I can find in him at this time is that he is not a Christian!"

If at that moment I could Skype this girl, the only sound she would hear would be a screaming Mimi over the Internet! Here is one of the replies I sent to a young girl who was defending her "religious" boyfriend.

Dear K_____:

Fasten your seatbelt...I care too much about you to not share the truth.

How ironic that you went to a secular college to be a witness for Jesus and now you are missionary dating. The key is not how nice your boyfriend is or how polite or how charming or unselfish or hardworking he is. There are thousands of religious people who have the same qualities. *Boaz* had all these qualities, but he had the most differentiating one: he loved the *Lord* and the *Word*, and *lived it.*

You said, "He is perfect for me, except for his lack of relationship with Jesus. Girlfriend, his relationship with *Jesus* is *all that matters!* The key is your boyfriend's love for Jesus, not his devotion to you. You know the difference, and you know that you are disobeying God's Word in Second Corinthians 6:14 and Amos 3:3. The reality is you are looking for permission to love someone who is charming but is not born again. You even admitted your fear of not finishing the race. Well, girlfriend, you are not running in your lane. You have already chosen your boyfriend over Jesus. That is why your friends have been trying to warn you to guard your heart.

The honorable thing would be for you to stop dating this guy, because he isn't born again. And he won't be born again by dating you, because you have accepted him as a charming nonbeliever, so *why should he change?!* Have you ever considered the reality that *you are standing* in the way of his coming to Jesus because you have "fogged up" the window of witness!?

If you *really love Jesus*, you wouldn't want to date a guy who isn't going to be a thriving, growing member of *Team Jesus*. Your nice guy isn't even on *Team Jesus*.

Sometimes I just want to cry because so many of God's girls are impatiently settling for guys who aren't growing Christians. As I grieve over so many of the e-mails I receive daily, I am reminded that *who* a gal loves is a "billboard" of her heart's condition spiritually. Gals who settle for Bozo guys or even very nice nonbelievers are displaying to the world their impatient hearts. Me-centric girls do not know how to be patient, and their appetite for instant gratification often results in vulnerability to Bozo guys!

Who a gal loves is a "billboard" of her heart's condition spiritually. Gals who settle for Bozo guys or even very nice nonbelievers are displaying to the world their impatient hearts.

LIVING NEXT DOOR TO HELL

Marriage to a non-Christian brings pain to the believing wife. A Christian counselor once described being married to a non-believer as moving next door to hell. As women, we long to be known and loved for all we are. A man who is spiritually dead can never know the very intimate spiritual part of you that is your heart. He would be blind to much of what you would try to share with him. He could never know and understand you fully.

Be careful when you begin to think that you are "in love" and you "just can't live without him." Think again. Think of the loneliness you will feel when your husband will not attend church with you. Think of the angry bickering that may take place between the two of you because he can never understand the depths of your spiritual awareness and, consequently, your convictions. If you do not think about this now, you may one day think, "Before, I couldn't live without him; now I can hardly live with him." Second Corinthians 6:14-15 is very clear:

> *Do not be bound together with unbelievers; for what partnership have righteousness and lawlessness, or what fellowship has light with darkness? Or what harmony has Christ with Belial, or what has a believer in common with an unbeliever?*

Please consider a greater consequence than being unhappily married to a man who does not know your Lord. Will you be able to handle the pain of watching your children live with possible rejection by their father, day in and day out? Will you think it is worth the cost when you are the only one who gets up on Sunday mornings to take your dear children to church?

Will it be worth the compromise when your children look up at you and ask why daddy doesn't love Jesus? They could even reject the Lord for eternity and live a miserable, ill-chosen lifestyle because of the choice you made to marry a wonderful, but lost, man. Children will often follow their father's example—good or bad. Exodus 34:7 gives a warning you cannot ignore: "*...He will by no means leave the guilty unpunished, visiting the iniquity of fathers on the children and on the grandchildren to the third and fourth generations.*" You are not just marrying a husband, but choosing a father for your children.

When you marry, you do not choose blessings or curses for you alone; you choose for the generations after you. If you choose to wait patiently for your knight in shining armor, you will be blessed by the heritage that a prince brings. If you choose to run eagerly ahead of God's plan and marry a man with no conscience toward God, you will reap the life's course he follows, but not alone. Your children's and grandchildren's lives will be directly affected by the man you marry.

Consider the following Scriptures:

All these blessings will come upon you and overtake you if you will obey the Lord your God (Deuteronomy 28:2).

But it shall come about, if you do not obey the Lord your God…all these curses shall come upon you and overtake you (Deuteronomy 28:15).

God warned His people in Deuteronomy of the long-term effects of their choices. Today other countries may not take our children, but there are many bondages in our wicked generation that could hold them.

Your sons and your daughters shall be given to another people, while your eyes look on and yearn for them continually; but there will be nothing you can do (Deuteronomy 28:32).

Have you seen the yearning eyes of a mother as she sees her son on drugs or her daughter living on the streets? There is nothing she can do but look on in pain.

These verses in Deuteronomy show that God has always desired to bless His people, but He will not force them to do what is best. In His Word He has often warned us to wait, to be careful, and to trust Him. He will not make us wait. His heart of love begs us to listen and obey so He may bless us and the dear ones who will one day look to and follow us. The words He gave to the children of Israel in Deuteronomy 30:15-20 show the love and concern He has for the choices you make.

So choose life in order that you may live, you and your descendants, by loving the Lord your God, by obeying His voice, and by holding fast to Him… (Deuteronomy 30:19-20).

You must choose to wait patiently for God's best. If you have seen patterns in your life that show a lack of patience, commit yourself right now to waiting for God's best.

You may pray something like this:

Lord, You are my sovereign God. You know all about me and love me more than anyone else ever could. You know how I feel, what I need, and what my future is. I confess that I have taken matters into my own hands. I confess to being afraid of totally trusting You. Today I commit myself to focus on You and Your love for me. Today I commit to look to You for my future—not to my outward circumstances. Thank You for knowing how weak I feel, but being strong for me and in me. I love You. I choose to trust You.

You may have to repeat this prayer, or one like it, many times when you feel afraid. But Psalm 103:13-14 assures us that He understands and has compassion on us:

Just as a father has compassion on his children, so the Lord has compassion on those who fear Him. For He Himself knows our frame; He is mindful that we are but dust.

DEVELOPING PATIENCE

Kimmy expressed that her focus was set and patience began in a real way in her life when, during her late twenties, she surrendered her life to Jesus. She said, "I remember telling the Lord, 'I don't care if I ever get married, I just want to love You, please You, and know You.' From that time I had a new peace and power. I got involved by ministering to the youth in my church and found joy in serving others. One girl told me her mother thought I was absolutely crazy, being as old as I was, to spend my time with the youth instead of trying to find a husband."

Kimmy served the Lord faithfully and contentedly alone until years later when Lynn recognized her as the lady God had for him. They were soon married because they had patiently used their waiting time to get ready.

Kimmy said, "God didn't supply all my wants when I was single. He changed my wants and supplied all my needs, better than I could have imagined."

One older single woman struggling to be a Lady in Waiting cried out to the Lord as to why He was delaying the coming of her knight. She searched her heart, thinking there must be something horribly amiss in her life for God to spend so many extra years developing her into a princess suitable for her knight-to-be. Her self-image began to suffer as she mentally blamed herself for the delays. Tenderly the Father gave her a verse she could cling to: *"Dwell in the land and cultivate faithfulness"* (Ps. 37:3).

She didn't really understand all that it meant, but chose to believe she was being all she should be before the Lord. As she began to dwell upon the positive things the Lord said about her in His Word, like *"the King's daughter is all glorious within"* (Ps. 45:13), she was able to reject negative, condemning thoughts and feelings, and choose to be the woman He wanted her to be as a single.

Little did she know that God needed those days to perfect her Boaz. We, as women, are not the only ones who need the days of waiting in order to be perfected for a future life-mate. Her knight had not been a Christian long, and in his spiritual immaturity would not have been a proper spiritual leader. He needed time to be grounded in the Word and to experience complete freedom over the sins of his past.

When the two of them were finally introduced, she understood why she had to wait. While she cultivated faithfulness before God, her knight had been slaying a few dragons and shining his armor. God did not leave her waiting any longer than necessary. She desired a knight, but patiently waited on God's timing. The two of them now glorify God in a ministry to drug and alcohol abusers.

Wait patiently. Perhaps you are giving God time to prepare, not yourself, but your beloved. Let your heavenly Father accomplish His work thoroughly while your single man is undistracted. Issues settled in a person's life while single limit unnecessary stress and difficulty later in a marriage. Psalm 37:7 says, *"Rest in the Lord and wait patiently for Him...."* Wait not for a man or a preconceived perfect future, but for Him. Verses 3, 4, and 5 of Psalm 37 give some great action words for the Lady of Patience to follow in order to wait before Him.

SPIRITUAL MONITORS THAT ENCOURAGE PATIENCE

I know a dear girl who was raised with an incredible spiritual legacy, yet was deeply hurt during a breakup with an awesome Christian guy. As I listened to the details of their dating relationship I clearly heard—*"no spiritual* monitor.*"* I know there was a lot said about spiritual monitors in Chapter 8, but it bears repeating, and *remembering* as a critical tool in developing patience!

This precious girl did not have anyone cautioning her not to outrun what God intended for this dating relationship. They were discussing marriage early in their dating journey. Everyone around them talked about them being the perfect couple. Now this all may seem pretty innocent, but honestly it was premature enthusiasm and assumption on the part of all the "older people" commenting on the couple's dating.

The encouragement of a spiritual monitor would have helped this young woman enact the Eleventh Commandment: *Thou shalt not defraud thyself.*

If you run ahead of a relationship, either emotionally or logistically, you run a high risk of being defrauded. And sadly, this "enhanced heartbreak" is a self-created suffering.

Over and over again I have seen that the girls who do not have spiritual monitors in their lives are the ones prone to enhancing their own heartbreak. What these girls did have was a cheering crowd that would end up *stunned* when the "perfect couple" broke up. Yet, the cheering crowds don't do a good job comforting heartbroken girls; and worse, they don't realize they were part of the problem in the first place!

Cheering with caution is the best thing any friend or parent can do for a friend or daughter who is dating. And girlfriend, *you* can be responsible to ask for that kind of encouragement! You can help the people around you know how best to cheer you on.

James 4 has a wonderful reminder for all of us concerning our dreamy ideas and runaway feelings:

Now listen, you who say, ["I know this is the one for me" or], *"Today or tomorrow we will go to this or that city, spend a year there, carry on business and make money." Why, you do not even know what will happen tomorrow. What is your life? You are* **a mist** *that appears for a little while and then vanishes. Instead, you ought to say,* **"If it is the Lord's will***, we will live and do this or that"* (James 4:13-15 NIV).

Most gals do not want to hear, *"If it is the Lord's will."* I am not advocating that you play "Deputy Downer" in your friend's life after every date. But I *am* suggesting that you consider this special role of a loving spiritual monitor who is looking for the right time to mention this key: that only Papa God knows whether this is a lifelong love or a friendship "tutorial" in your understanding the difference between a Boaz and a Bozo, between Mr. Right and Mr. Wrong.

Although a present crush or dating relationship can evaporate like a mist just as quickly as it arrived, nothing is wasted in the emotional tutorial of a gal's heart.

A FABULOUS GUY, BUT ON HIS BEST DAY... STILL A MAN

One of the biggest surprises for so many single women who wait for God's best and finally marry a modern Boaz is that they are shocked when they discover (even on their honeymoons) that they have married *mere men*. I tell women all the time, "My husband is a great guy, but he is a lousy god!" When I look to my husband to be anything more than a faithful yet flawed man, I am setting myself up for disappointment.

When a woman wants her husband to be her source of love, joy, peace, etc., she puts immeasurable pressure on the husband. God never intended for a man to be everything a woman needed (or vice versa)—that is an idolatrous mentality that doesn't sit well with our heavenly Bridegroom. The more a woman discovers that Jesus is her Source, the more she removes such pressure from her husband.

Talking with a young woman who just celebrated her first year of marriage, I was so impressed with her joy and success. I couldn't even comprehend such a great first year. My first year of marriage, though I was married to a classic Boaz, had so much heartache for me. Why? I had mentally constructed a list of expectations that no man could ever measure up to. I wanted my early years of marriage to be a "ten," but I did not take into account the "five" world we were living in. I kept forgetting that Ken and I did not move into the Garden of Paradise when we got married.

We are still living outside the Garden in a very challenging world full of opportunities for disappointment and even disillusionment. I have heard it said, "You can tell a lot about people's spiritual maturity by noting their response to chaos. Mature Christians have learned that life is more chaotic than predictable." Recognizing this reality will help any man or woman maneuver the rough waters of life.

Loving a flawed man for a lifetime requires that you understand the ebb and flow of love. Mature love understands that on some days, one's love is like high tide, and on other days, it's more like low tide. A flawed though faithful man will be a journey partner who is learning how to live unselfishly during the high and low tides of life.

Remember, your Boaz will allow you to continue in the direction of your life adventure designed by God. He will allow you to stay in your "lane" and finish the race set before you. He will be a lifelong dancing partner even if he knows he has two left feet.[2]

Marriage is every bit as much work as it is wonderful, even in God's way and time. It is good, but don't be deceived into mistaking it for Heaven.

Realizing that marriage is not a dream but real life can also help you to wait more patiently. Instead of merely being envious, get with a godly married woman and see the extra load she carries. Look at all she cannot do, instead of the fact that she has a man in her house. Understand that in reality, married life is not constant communication, daily roses, hugs and kisses, breakfast in bed, and sheer bliss. Marriage is every bit as much work as it is wonderful, even in God's way and time. It is good, but don't be deceived into mistaking it for Heaven.

Since no spouse is perfect, learning to live "as one" is not without its tears. Marriage alone is not a cure-all or answer to every heartfelt need. If you think it is, you had better just keep waiting, for that kind of marriage doesn't exist. Although there is a romantic inside every one of us, you must be realistic regarding marriage, or the shock could be devastating.

"Another thing that helped me wait patiently," Kimmy wrote, "was a sense of humor. Laugh about 'always a bridesmaid but never a bride.' Joke about opening your own attendant shop because you have so many bridesmaid dresses. Talk about being single with others in a fun way, not with a 'woe is me' attitude."

Find other single girls and plan activities. Don't just sit at home on Friday night. Go out to eat, or to the movies, and become involved working with children, young people, or senior adults. There are many things you can do to stay busy and keep from becoming impatient.

MISSED OUT—WHILE WAITING

My best friend was single until she was forty (yes!—a forty-year-old virgin). Twenty years ago I wrote about her in Chapter 3 *Lady of Faith*. During her prolonged, God-scripted singleness when she recounted to me about some Bozo guy who hurt someone she knew, I would always respond, "Consider all the Bozo guys you have been *spared!*"

During her singleness, she witnessed so many tragic choices single women made that her patience was actually strengthened by seeing so many "good" bad examples of what to avoid!

Another very wise, single friend who is having a somewhat prolonged single journey wrote about what she has *missed* while waiting for God's best and staying a virgin as she waits:

> [People] deeply underestimate the power of sex. It was not designed by God as a casual act to be shared indiscriminately with anyone and everyone. It was devised by our Creator as the healthy by-product of a healthy marriage, not the objective of a relationship. It was for this reason I made a commitment as a preteen to honor my future husband all the days of my life. I am still waiting, and when people suggest I have "missed out," I can agree: *I have missed out on heartbreak, insecurities relating to my body, sharing the most precious part of my heart with someone other than my husband, STDs, unplanned pregnancy, etc.* (emphasis added).[3]

PROTECTED, NOT REJECTED

A post on Beth Moore's Living Proof Ministries blog by her Media Assistant, Lindsee Eddy, highlighted an incredibly important principle for any Lady in Waiting to fully grasp:

> What I do want you to know is that those boys not pursuing me is not a reflection of me whatsoever. It's not because I'm fat, or ugly, or don't dress cute enough, or am not outgoing enough, or am not godly enough, or whatever reason we girls can come up with. I truly believe it is the Lord protecting my heart.

> Although it could be easily labeled as rejection, it's simply the Lord's protection. At least that's how I've seen it.

> I don't know why He's chosen to protect my heart for so long. I do know that it's His grace in my life. I do know He alone has spared me from many broken hearts. I do know that He is building in me something beautiful. I do know that He is sanctifying me through and through and molding me into the woman I am to be one day to my

future husband. However future that may be. I do know that marriage is a legitimate desire of my heart that I believe He's placed there and that He will be faithful.

I might not be able to testify to the girls about the amazing man the Lord had blessed me with, but I am able to testify about His faithfulness despite my circumstances. He is good.

I know that I have rejected not one date, nor has the Lord ever rejected my heart, my desires, or me. And He won't reject yours, either.[4]

May God make you a cheerleader for your single friends, reminding them what they are *not missing* and reminding them of being *protected, not rejected.* Of course your primary cheer for all singles, whatever age and stage of life— "No Bozos! Only a Boaz!"

Developing patience is hard. Getting married ahead of God's timing is worse. God may not work according to your time schedule, but He does have your best interests in mind. One single said, "As a teenager, I had my life all planned out. I would meet my husband at age 19, marry at 21, and start my family at 23. These were my plans, but evidently not God's plans for my life. I am 41 now, but enjoy a wonderful single life."

You don't know what tomorrow holds, but you do know who holds tomorrow. Say this with the psalmist:

> *O Lord, my heart is not proud, nor my eyes haughty; nor do I involve myself in great matters, or in things too difficult for me. Surely I have composed and quieted my soul; like a weaned child rests against his mother, my soul is like a weaned child within me. O* [substitute your name], *hope in the Lord from this time forth and forever* (Psalm 131).

The place of rest that the psalmist found was a result of the choice he made. This quietness of soul did not come naturally to him. He actively chose to take himself out of involvement and quiet his soul (his mind, will, and emotions). He chose to put his hope in God.

Are you trying to involve yourself in matters that are too great for you? Can you see into a man's heart? Can you know the future? You know Someone who does know men's hearts and the future. Patiently rest against His chest. He will bring you the peace you need. This attitude of patience is not something that will just happen. By an act of your will you must choose to trust God regardless of what happens. Patiently wait for His best.

You know Someone who knows men's hearts and the future. Patiently rest against His chest.

Every single woman must at some point come to grips with the fact that not all women will marry. Marriage is not a need, though God chooses to let marriage meet some needs a woman may have. Marriage is not a right, though God chooses to plan marriage for the majority of women. Marriage does not complete a person, though women who properly marry find that marriage rounds out some of their weaknesses. If marriage were a need, right, or completion for women, then all godly women would marry. There are many examples of true, God-honoring women who had no earthly mate but were still Ladies of Patience.

One Lady in Waiting wrote this:

I believe part of being a Lady of Patience is honestly facing the future. For me that was realizing that I might not ever get married.

I could handle the thoughts of "waiting on the Lord," but to face the reality that it may not be His desire for me to marry was hard to cope with. As I read my Bible, I found Isaiah 54:5. The verse said I was already married to Him. He was my Husband! I was His bride. He wanted me to know Him, my Husband. He wanted me to see myself as His bride, to know His love for me. He wanted to be intimate with me. So I began my walk with my Husband, the Lord Jesus.

I still desire to get married; in fact, many times I have longed for a husband and even cried for one. There have been times when I thought I had met "the one for me," then was terribly disappointed. But I always knew I could go back to my Husband who understood my desire and my hurts. He would encourage me by showing me His love in even deeper ways.

GUARD AGAINST THE LIE THAT ONLY SINGLES ARE LONELY

In the mid-1800s, a lovely single woman wrote to author Hannah Whitall Smith about her struggle with loneliness and depression. You may have heard Hannah's name before—she wrote the classic *The Christian's Secret of a Happy Life*. The answer she gave her lonely friend is just as relevant now as it was in the 19th century.

The loneliness thou speaks of I know all about. For do not think, darling, that it is confined to unmarried people. It is just as real in lives that have plenty of human ties: husbands and children and friends.... And I believe God very rarely allows any human love to be satisfying, just that this loneliness may drive us to Himself. I have noticed that where a human love is satisfying, something always comes in to spoil it. Either there is a death, or there are separations, or there is change of feeling on one side or the other, or something, and the heart is driven out of its human resting place.[5]

An e-mail I received from a single gal named Keren living in the Middle East reminded me of what Hannah wrote. She clearly understands the commitment required from a single woman who wants to guard her heart and follow her God. Keren wrote:

I can read the Bible a hundred times, read *Lady in Waiting* fifty times, but if my heart is not ready to give away to Him my desires, nothing in the world will help. Therefore it is for those who are ready to give the King all their dreams, desires, and wishes and go with their "Naomis" to the unknown [that they will find] in the end God's Promised Land. [Such following may] look good to us or not—but God, His ways are perfect, and He protects those who hide under the shadow of His wings. We must trust God during our time of waiting, during moments of loneliness, and must fight the best we can (with God's help) to guard our hearts, for from our hearts come the issues of life.

Hannah Whitall Smith went one step further in her letter to the single woman, to remind her—and all of us, single, married, widowed, divorced—that the ultimate answer is not in Mr. Right but in a right relationship with God. In this excerpt, Hannah addressed the timeless reality that *God is enough*.

No soul can be really at rest until it has given up all dependence on everything else and has been forced to depend on the Lord alone. As long as our expectation is from other things, nothing but disappointment awaits us. Feelings may change, and will change, with our changing circumstances: doctrines and dogmas may be upset; Christian work may come to naught; prayers may seem to lose their fervency; promises may seem to fail; everything that we have believed in or depended upon may seem to be swept away, and only God is left, just God, the bare God, if I may be allowed the expression; simply and only God....

This, then, is what I mean by God being enough. It is that we find in Him, the fact of His existence and of His character, all that we can possibly want for everything. God is, must be, our answer to every question and every cry of need. If there is any lack in the One who has undertaken to save us, nothing supplementary we can do will avail to make it up; and if there is no lack in Him, then He of Himself and in Himself is enough.[6]

...only God is left, just God, the bare God, if I may be allowed the expression; simply and only God...
This, then, is what I mean by God being enough.

IMPATIENCE: THE PEN WRITING POST-DATED CHECKS FOR MARITAL UNFAITHFULNESS

I met once with a single girl at Starbucks to discuss a few of her heart's questions. As I listened to her Mr. Bozo story, something she said sent me scrambling for a piece of paper to record it. This beautiful young woman explained, "I grew up being the good girl. I was a good girl in high school and a good girl in college. But after I graduated, *I violated my own values.*"

I asked her if she understood why she violated the values she had so strongly clung to all the way through school. Her immediate reply was, "Jackie, because of impatience with God, I felt that God had not delivered my Mr. Right…so I wasn't waiting any longer."

She described a relationship with a typical Bozo whom she knew deep in her heart was not God's best. She went on to elaborate on her rationalizing that other young people were living together. She thought, "So what's the big deal?"

Impatience propelled this young woman into the arms of a Bozo.

This beautiful young woman explained, "I grew up being the good girl. I was a good girl in high school and a good girl in college. But after I graduated, I violated my own values."

Here is a principle that so many young people want to remain oblivious to: the worst thing about having sex or fooling around physically before marriage is the vulnerability it leads to after marriage. When you fool around after marriage, it's even more costly. It's called adultery, and it wreaks havoc on marriages and families and even whole communities!

To remain pure prior to marriage is unquestionably a struggle, but singles think the struggle is because they're not married. What is so critical for single gals to understand is this: If you cannot control yourself sexually before marriage, you will likely not do so after marriage. I have never interviewed one person whose husband has been unfaithful who did not struggle and fool around with him before marriage. Sexual self-control is developed *this* side of marriage.

This is not to say that God cannot redeem sexual appropriateness within marriage for people who have been sexually active prior to matrimony. His grace enables us to grow in holiness at any stage of our spiritual development. But this takes intentional commitment and an understanding of how premarital sex affects the marriage relationship.

Without that conviction, however, sexual impurity before marriage is likely to be a post-dated check for immorality within marriage. That is called *adultery.* The gold ring on the left hand does not instantly transform us; we bring into marriage what we practiced before marriage.

Another single woman named Beverly developed the following Bible study to calm the impatience of her heart.

Why Do I Want to Get Married? By Beverly Seward Brandon

Why Do I Want to Get Married?	How Can God Meet Those Needs in My Life?
I want to be loved.	"*I have loved you with an everlasting love*" (Jer. 31:3).
I want someone to adore me.	The King has brought me into His chambers to adore me. My lover is outstanding among 10,000 (see Song of Solomon 1:4; 5:10).
I want someone to hold my hand.	"*I will uphold you with My righteous right hand*" (Isa. 41:10).
I want to be accepted and valued.	I am accepted in the Beloved (see Eph. 1:6 KJV).
I want a "place," a nesting place that is my own to create and use.	We can rest in the shadow of the Almighty (see Ps. 91:1).
I want help in my days of trouble.	"*Call upon Me in the day of trouble; I shall rescue you*" (Ps. 50:15).

(continued)

Why Do I Want to Get Married?	How Can God Meet Those Needs in My Life?
I want to share my life—the joys and the struggles—with one person (intimacy).	God will share with me the treasures of darkness and hidden riches (see Isa. 45:3).
I want a champion of my causes—one who is willing to fight for me.	*"The Lord will fight for you"* (Exod. 14:14).
I want someone to meet my needs.	God is meeting all my needs (see Phil. 4:19).
I want intimacy.	The Lord is intimate with the upright (see Ps. 140:13).
I want someone to help me in my life.	There is no one like God who rides the heavens to help you (see Deut. 33:26).
I want to walk through life sustained and carried. I don't want the whole load of life.	Even to my old age, God will sustain me, carry me, and rescue me (see Isa. 46:4).
I want a companion for this life.	God invites us to humbly walk with Him (see Mic. 6:8).
I desire children.	God gives us spiritual children like the numberless grains of sand if we invest in lives (see Isa. 48:19).

Beverly's response to this study: "The Lord, my Maker, is my Husband. Only He can meet the deepest needs of my heart. No man can ever come through for me fully. Only He can. He is what I long for. Only God is enough."

PATIENTLY WAITING: HOW WILL I KNOW HIM?

One day our daughter was wondering out loud how she would know which guy was the best for her. I spontaneously shared the following, and it has been shared with many others since.

I told her that God's best for her would always complement the direction God wanted her to go. It is like a big running track with freshly painted lanes. As she takes off running in her lane, relentlessly in pursuit of Jesus, the guy who will complement her journey will arrive someday in this manner: She will be just running in her lane, looking ahead, when all of a sudden she will hear this deep panting, and suddenly alongside her in the next lane she will hear someone approaching. She will not have to stop running, she will not have to change her pace, and she won't have to look behind her, because before she knows it, he will be running alongside her. He will keep up with her, and they will continue the race at a complementary pace.

This will be her running partner for the journey ahead. They will encourage each other and not trip each other. I have met too many women who are running a fabulous race when suddenly they are tripped up by some Bozo guy shouting for her to slow down, take a break on the benches with him, and she is sidetracked for years by him.

Remember to be patient in anticipation of one coming up alongside you, who will also be panting in relentless pursuit of Jesus.

Regardless of what you see or what you feel, God is in full control of your situation. You, Lady in Waiting, can walk in victory by choosing to be patient in your wait.

GUARD AGAINST WANTING SOMEONE ELSE'S BOAZ

Too often when a single gal has been very patient for an extended period of time, she is more vulnerable than ever when she *finally meets a Boaz*. He may have just moved into the circle of friends you associate with daily. He may have been transferred into your office or workplace. He may have been invited as a guest to your singles' Bible study. No matter how he arrives—even if it is on a white horse and he's wearing Knight's Armor Cologne—you still must guard your heart against the ever-prevalent assumption that he is "the" Boaz you have been waiting for!

After your first conversation with this modern Boaz, the moment you're alone, you need to put your hand over your heart and say the Single Woman's Pledge of Allegiance (cited at the end of Chapter 8). You need to make yourself accountable to a friend. You need to devote yourself to prayer about the great man you have just met.

You may think I'm recommending extreme reactions. "If he's a Boaz," you reason, "why not just grab him?" To guard your heart when "Mr. Right" arrives within ten feet of you may seem unnecessary, but countless women have lived with the deepest of heart wounds because they assumed that a great guy was *the* Mr. Right. *Just because he is a Boaz doesn't mean he is your Boaz.*

And if he's not meant to be *your* Boaz, what a blessing it is to align with God's will in praying for the woman who *is* meant for this guy. Not only is this a service to that sister in Christ (whom you may never even know!) but it veers you away from the temptation to "posses" this Boaz in your own thoughts. Whenever you find yourself lured into vain imaginings (fantasies) about your next encounter with him, STOP and pray for the gal who *is* being prepared for this guy. This kind of prayer is the best kind of heart guard!

Right before I left for college, a young man spoke at our home Bible study. We were all so impressed with this good-looking guy, who was not ashamed of his passion for God. That night several of us left the study with a bit of a crush on this godly young man. He was an obvious Boaz.

When I returned to college, I was stunned to find a letter from him. He began to write to me regularly. His deep love for God permeated his letters. After writing me for several months, he came to visit me at college in Chattanooga. I was so nervous, because I knew what an incredible guy he was, and I honestly was shocked by his interest in me.

He stayed with a guy friend of mine in the men's dorm, and we spent every free moment throughout the weekend together. Just before he was ready to return to his job in Atlanta, we took a walk and he said, "Jackie, I have been praying for months and I have spoken with my parents about this—I believe that you are the woman I have been waiting for all these years." He said he would drive back to see me in three weeks and I could tell him how I felt about him at that time.

Less than twenty-four hours later, I was thinking about our time together and what an incredible guy he was. While I was praying, I heard, "Yes, he is incredible, but he is not your Boaz." I recommitted myself to God's plan, and I immediately wrote and told the young man he didn't need to return in three weeks. I told him that God showed me clearly that he was not my Boaz. In fact, I closed my letter with this comment: "Adam, go back to sleep, your Eve is not ready yet."

That may seem harsh, but wait 'til you hear the rest of the story.

With my rejection of this Boaz's proposal, he agreed to join the God's Smuggler team with its leader, Brother Andrew, in Europe. This group smuggled Bibles into Communist countries when it was illegal—and very dangerous— to do so. For ten years, this Boaz served with that team. His singleness was a great advantage. He could serve with Brother Andrew in hazardous situations without worries about a wife and children. The inherent risks that came daily with this particular work would have put enormous pressure on any team member who was married.

I said no to Boaz, and he was free to take risks serving the Lord he loved so desperately.

I said no to Boaz, and he was free to take risks serving the Lord he loved so desperately. Yes, he was a Boaz, but he was not mine, and I was not his Ruth. After serving for ten years, he returned to Atlanta where he finally married his Ruth.

I eventually met my Boaz, Ken, and married him. The next time you meet an obvious Boaz, pray that he finds his Ruth—even if it is not you.[7]

Don't let your impatient longings rob you of the life God wants to bless you—or your Christian brothers—with as a single. Realize you do not need marriage for happiness or a full life. If you are holding on to marriage as a right, relinquish this right so it will not keep you from God's fullest blessings.

God knows what is best for you. His timing is perfect, and He will take care of His Lady of Patience.

Final Word from Jackie: Listen to Your Heavenly Papa

In June 1996, I heard Steven Spielberg being interviewed about his work with Holocaust survivors. He brought out a woman named Gerta, one of the few women who survived the Death March during World War II. The march went from Poland to Czechoslovakia; it was three hundred miles and three months long.

Gerta told an astounding story. She recounted that one afternoon in the concentration camp in Poland, she was told that all the women were going on a walk. Just before leaving, her father called to her across the courtyard and yelled, "Gerta, put on your boots!"

It was June and all the young girls were barefoot, including Gerta. But, being a good Jewish girl, she knew not to argue with Papa. So there was Gerta, putting on boots in June to take a walk, assuming, of course, she would return to camp.

This obedient young woman survived what turned out to be a three-month ordeal because she listened to her papa. She watched the other girls breaking off their toes like twigs as their feet froze at night. Gerta watched hundreds die from their feet upward—as she survived in her boots.

What an extraordinary story of the simplest, yet most profound provision by God. Gerta's story is a challenge to all of "Papa's children" (see Gal. 4:6). Our heavenly Father knows the march we are on, and He alone knows what is ahead for each of us. So when He gives us instruction—even when it doesn't make sense (see Isa. 55:8-9)—we need to listen to Papa. This swift obedience is certainly part of our reckless abandon to Him.

Let's consider some basic instructions from Papa. Which of them are "boots in June" for you?

The Lady in Waiting

Recklessly abandon's herself to the Lordship of Christ,
Diligently uses her single days,
Trusts God with unwavering faith,
Demonstrates virtue in daily life,
Loves God with undistracted devotion,
Stands for physical and emotional purity,
Lives in security,
Responds to life in contentment,
Makes choices based on her convictions,
And waits patiently for God to meet her needs.

These are your "boots in June"! Put them on now girlfriend—so the road ahead will be the beginning and not the end for you.

BECOMING A LADY OF PATIENCE

- Write out the things that make you lose patience. Which of these cause your Sovereign God concern? Give these concerns to Him and ask Him to help you trust while you wait. "I will trust while I wait, for my God is never late" is a good motto.

- How often do you impatiently pursue what your Father wants to give you as you are sitting still? (See Isaiah 64:4.)

- How often do you panic and conclude that God is not going to provide a Boaz for you? (See Matthew 6:25-33.)

- How often do you assume what God is going to do next and rush ahead, fearful that it will not satisfy you? Are you trying to help God find your Mr. Right?

- How many times have you suffered because you assumed what God would do and then you were knocked down by the surprising turn of events? (See Isaiah 55:8.)

- Discuss this idea: Just because he is a Boaz doesn't mean he's *your* Boaz.

- Have you ever assumed a Boaz was yours? What happened when you realized you were wrong?

- Read Second Samuel 13:1-16 and thoroughly examine the Bozo that Amnon was…his name in Hebrew means "Trustworthy." How ironic! Another man who did not live his name. Too many Christian guys are men who do not live their name!

- Discuss: Fabulous Guy but on His Best Day Still a Man. Loving our faithful but flawed men—ponder!

- Read Deuteronomy 28:1-48. Write on one side of a piece of paper the blessings God wanted the nation of Israel to have as His children. Write on the other side what He asked them to do. What does He require of you?

- Read Deuteronomy 28:1-48 again. Write the curses that came from choosing to be disobedient to God. Confess any ways that you have chosen to disobey God's will for your life.

- Read Deuteronomy 30 and write down all the tender ways God spoke to His children, trying to help them choose what was best. How can you commit today to remain true to your loving Father and patiently wait? Look at the way He understands how His children feel in verses 11-14.

- Make Psalm 27 your prayer and commit it, or another passage, to memory to use on those hard days.

ENDNOTES

1. Eloise Salholz, "Too Late for Prince Charming?" Newsweek, June 2, 1986.

2. Kendall, *A Man Worth Waiting For*, 147–149.

3. Ibid., 208–209.

4. Ibid., 212–213.

5. Ibid.

6. Ibid.

7. Ibid., 208–209.

SUGGESTED READINGS

Eros Defiled by John White

Too Close, Too Soon by Jim Talley and Bobbie Reed

Passion and Purity by Elisabeth Elliot

The Pursuit of God by A.W. Tozer

Finding God by Dr. Larry Crabb

Search for Significance by Robert McGee

Trusting God by Jerry Bridges

We are the sum total of what we have read.
If you would like a list of my favorite books, e-mail me:
Jackie@jackiekendall.com

About Jackie Kendall and Debby Jones

Both authors are available for speaking engagements.

For more information, call or write:

Jackie Kendall

PO Box 220836

West Palm Beach, FL 33422-0836

Phone: 1.561.689.6082

E-mail: jackie@jackiekendall.com

Website: www.jackiekendall.com

Debby Jones

Crossover Communications International

PO Box 211755

Columbia, SC 29221

Phone: 1.803.691.0688

Help for Finding God's Best in a Mate

How to Avoid a Bozo —Jackie Kendall

Why are so many Christians making such poor choices in life-mates? Do you want to find God's best—Mr. Right? Learn from this video the differences between a man worth waiting for and a Bozo. Discover how to avoid the counterfeit and find the real thing!

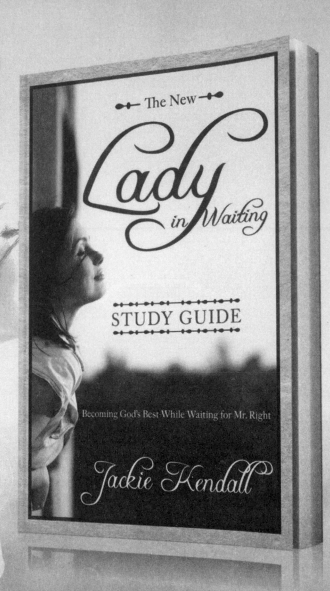

The New

Lady

in Waiting

STUDY GUIDE

Becoming God's Best While Waiting for Mr. Right

Jackie Kendall

Be sure to pick up the Study Guide at
your favorite bookstore or online at
ChurchAlly.com
for your small or large group.

❤📖 LOVE to READ?

Get FREE eBooks,
Deep Discounts and New Release Updates!
Sign up now.
destinyimage.com/freebooks

📑 SHARE this BOOK!

Don't let the impact of this book end with you!
Get a discount
when you order
3 or MORE BOOKS.
CALL 1-888-987-7033

🎤 AUTHOR INTERVIEWS

Exclusive interviews with your favorite authors!
Tune in today.
voiceofdestiny.net

 Destiny Image is a division of Nori Media Group.